craft tree

Easy Crocheted Accessories

COMPILED BY **Amy Palmer**

INTERWEAVE.
interweave.com

The projects in this collection were originally published in other Interweave publications, including Interweave Crochet, Interweave Knits, Knitscene, *and* Piecework *magazines and* CrochetMe *eBooks. Some have been altered to update information and/or conform to space limitations.*

Interweave Press LLC,
a division of F+W Media Inc
201 East Fourth Street
Loveland, CO 80537
interweave.com

Printed in the United States
by Versa Press

Table of Contents

The Road to Bruges
by Annette Petavy

In the nineteenth century, crochet was largely used to imitate traditional lace techniques, such as bobbin lace. One famous type of bobbin lace came from Bruges/Brügge, Belgium, and *crochet de Bruges* was developed to imitate it. The simple ribbonlike technique is well worth exploring with materials other than thin white cotton thread.

Finished Size
About 10½" × 69" (26.5 × 175 cm).

Yarn
Ornaghi Filati Merino Kind (100% wool; 137 yd [125 m]/1¾ oz [50 g]; (4)): #904, 4 balls. Yarn distributed by Aurora Yarns.

Hook
Size G/7 (4.5 mm). Adjust hook size if necessary to obtain correct gauge.

Notions
Yarn needle.

Gauge
9 rows of Bruges ribbon = 4" (10 cm); 4 dc = about 1" (2.5 cm).

-----

notes

* A snaking, narrow ribbon of solid sts with ch-6 arches on both sides is connected to itself and to the ribbon border by joining ch-arch to ch-arch. Beg with the snaking ribbon and lace body of the scarf, connecting arches with sl sts as you go. Finish with the long oval border. A split tr is used to join ch-arches at the long edges of the scarf.

* The Bruges ribbon should always lie flat; it is very important not to twist the ribbon as you work.

-----

stitch guide

Bruges ribbon
Ch 10.

Row 1: Dc in 7th ch from hook (6 ch count as ch-6 arch), dc in next 3 ch, turn—4 dc.

Row 2: Ch 6, dc in each dc across, turn. Rep Row 2.

Join ch-arches: Ch 3, sl st in indicated ch-arch, ch 3.

Split treble crochet (split tr)
Yo 2 times, insert hook in first ch-arch, yo and pull up lp (4 lps on hook), yo and draw through 2 lps on hook (3 lps on hook), yo, insert hook in 2nd ch-arch, yo and pull up lp (5 lps on hook), yo and draw through 2 lps on hook (4 lps on hook), yo and draw through 3 lps on hook, yo and draw through rem 2 lps on hook.

Scarf

Work Rows 1–2 of Bruges ribbon (see Stitch Guide). Rep Row 2 seven more times (9 rows total).

Curve

ROW 1: Ch 6, dc in first 2 sts, hdc in next st, sc in last st, turn.

ROW 2: Ch 1 (does not count as st), sc in first st, hdc in next st, dc in last 2 sts, turn.

Rep Rows 1–2 of curve 3 times. Rep Row 1—9 rows in curve.

*Cont in Bruges ribbon for 6 rows, joining ch-arches (see Stitch Guide) on Rows 1, 3, and 5 to the opposing ch-arches in the straight line of ribbon previously made. Beg curve as described above, attaching ch-arch on Row 1 of curve to opposing ch-arch. Finish curve without attaching any more ch-arches. Rep from * until 32 curves are completed. Work 6 rows of Bruges ribbon, joining the ch-arches on Rows 1, 3, and 5, cont in Bruges ribbon for 3 more rows, attaching the ch-arch on Row 7 (but not the ch-arch on Row 9). Fasten off.

Edging

The edging is an oval-shaped Bruges ribbon worked around the perimeter of the scarf. Join yarn at first curve after beg of ribbon on long side of scarf.

ROW 1: Ch 7 (counts as 4 base ch, 3 joining ch), sl st in center ch-arch of first curve, ch 3, dc in 7th st from hook, count (3 ch sts, 1 sl st and then 3 ch sts back to the closest base ch), dc in the closest base ch; dc in each of last 3 ch, turn.

ROW 2: Ch 6, dc in each dc of edging ribbon, turn—4 dc.

ROW 3: Ch 3, split tr (see Stitch Guide) over next 2 free ch-arches, ch 3, dc across, turn.

ROW 4: Ch 6, dc across, turn.

ROW 5: Ch 3, sl st in split tr from Row 3, ch 3, dc across ribbon, turn.

ROW 6: Rep Row 4.

ROW 7: Ch 3, sl st in next free ch-arch (center ch-arch of curve), ch 3, dc across ribbon, turn.

ROW 8: Rep Row 4.

Rep Rows 3–8 until last free ch-arch on first long side is joined, ending with Row 8.

First edging corner

ROW 1: Ch 3, dc bet 2nd and 3rd dc of short end of scarf ribbon, ch 3, dc in each dc of edging ribbon, turn.

ROW 2: Ch 6, dc in first 2 sts, hdc in next st, sc in last st, turn.

ROW 3: Ch 1 (does not count as st), sc in first st, hdc in next st, dc in last 2 sts, turn.

ROW 4: Ch 6, dc across, turn.

ROW 5: Ch 3, sl st in dc at outside corner of end of scarf ribbon, ch 3, dc in each dc of edging ribbon.

Rep Rows 2–3. Cont edging ribbon, joining next 5 ch-arches of short end of scarf ribbon.

Second corner

Work 2 rows of ribbon without joining ch-arches. You will have 1 free ch-arch on the inner side of edging ribbon. Rep Rows 2–3 of first edging corner. Work 1 row of ribbon.

NEXT ROW: Ch 3, split tr over previous free ch-arch of edging ribbon and next free ch-arch of scarf ribbon, ch 3, dc in each dc of edging ribbon. Rep Rows 2–3 of first edging corner. Cont ribbon along 2nd long side of scarf, working edging the same way as for first long side; the first ch-arch to be attached is the center ch-arch of the first curve. At end of long side, rep as for first and 2nd corner. Work 1 row of Bruges ribbon. Fasten off.

Finishing

With yarn and yarn needle, sew short ends of edging ribbon tog. Weave in loose ends. Soak scarf for about twenty minutes in tepid water. Pin to desired measurements. Let dry. 🖋

ANNETTE PETAVY lives and crochets near Lyon, France. Her website is www.annettepetavy.com.

Tips for Making Bruges Lace

- Don't twist the ribbon. Your work should lie flat at all times.

- Do experiment with different types of ribbon. It can be made wider or narrower and include openwork. One simple variation is a ribbon of 5 dc, where every other row is worked as foll: Dc in first dc, ch 1, sk next dc, dc in next dc, ch 1, sk next dc, dc in last dc, turn.

- The number of ch in the arches can be modified.

- Do explore different ways to attach the ch-arches. Find examples in books, magazines, or online.

- Work Bruges crochet with a self-striping yarn. The result can be stunning.

- Try drawing a simple figure on a large piece of paper and make the ribbon follow it to create your own unique Bruges design.

Julia's HAT
by Natasha Robarge

Julia's Hat is a feminine cloche that works up faster than you might think. The body of the hat is worked entirely in single crochet. Two layers of simple lace trim add the perfect touch of elegance. Whip up this beautiful warm hat for yourself or a gift this winter.

Finished Size
About 21" (53.5 cm) head circumference.

Yarn
Patons Classic Wool (100% wool; 223 yd [205 m]/3.5 oz [100 g]; (4)): #77532 cognac heather (A) and #77425 woodrose heather (B), 1 ball each.

Hook
Size H/8 (5 mm). Adjust hook size if necessary to obtain correct gauge.

Notions
Stitch markers (m); yarn needle.

Gauge
15 sts and 19 rows = 4" (10 cm) in sc.

---

notes

* Hat is crocheted from top to bottom in a spiral without joining rnds in this order: flat top, shaped crown, straight sides, and flared brim.
* Place marker (pm) in first st of rnd to mark beg; move m up each rnd.
* Beg of rnds will shift to the right. Incs are staggered to avoid angles.

Hat

Flat circular top

With A, make adjustable ring (see Glossary). 6 sc in ring. Pull yarn tail to tighten ring. Cont sc in a spiral (see Notes), do not join.

RND 1: 2 sc in each sc around—12 sc.

RND 2: 2 sc in first sc, [sc in next sc, 2 sc in next sc] 5 times, sc in last sc—18 sc.

RND 3: Sc in first 2 sc, [2 sc in next sc, sc in next 2 sc] 5 times, 2 sc in last sc—24 sc.

RND 4: Sc in first sc, [2 sc in next sc, sc in next 3 sc] 5 times, 2 sc in next sc, sc in last 2 sc—30 sc.

RND 5: 2 sc in first sc, [sc in next 4 sc, 2 sc in next sc] 5 times, sc in next 4 sc—36 sc.

RND 6: Sc in first 4 sc, [2 sc in next sc, sc in next 5 sc] 5 times, 2 sc in next sc, sc in last sc—42 sc.

RND 7: Sc in first 2 sc, [2 sc in next sc, sc in next 6 sc] 5 times, 2 sc in next sc, sc in last 4 sc—48 sc.

RND 8: 2 sc in first sc, [sc in next 7 sc, 2 sc in next sc] 5 times, sc in next 7 sc—54 sc.

RND 9: Sc in first 7 sc, [2 sc in next sc, sc in next 8 sc] 5 times, 2 sc in next sc, sc in last sc—60 sc.

RND 10: Sc in first 4 sc, [2 sc in next sc, sc in next 9 sc] 5 times, 2 sc in next sc, sc in last 5 sc—66 sc.

Shape crown

RND 1: Sc around—66 sc.

RND 2: Sc in first sc, [2 sc in next sc, sc in next 10 sc] 5 times, 2 sc in next sc, sc in last 9 sc—72 sc.

RND 3: Sc around.

RND 4: Sc in first 9 sc, [2 sc in next sc, sc in next 11 sc] 5 times, 2 sc in next sc, sc in last 2 sc—78 sc.

RNDS 5–20: Sc around.

Try on hat to confirm desired depth. Work more rnds if necessary and, once hat is desired length, pm in last rnd.

Shape brim

RND 1: 2 sc in first sc, [sc in next 12 sc, 2 sc in next sc] 5 times, sc in next 12 sc—84 sc.

RND 2: Sc in first 5 sc, [2 sc in next sc, sc in next 13 sc] 5 times, 2 sc in next sc, sc in last 8 sc—90 sc.

RND 3: Sc in first 10 sc, [2 sc in next sc, sc in next 14 sc] 5 times, 2 sc in next sc, sc in last 4 sc—96 sc.

RND 4: Sc in first 3 sc, [2 sc in next sc, sc in next 15 sc] 5 times, 2 sc in next sc, sc in last 12 sc—102 sc.

RND 5: Sc in first 9 sc, [2 sc in next sc, sc in next 16 sc] 5 times, 2 sc in next sc, sc in last 7 sc—108 sc.

RND 6: Sc in first sc, [2 sc in next sc, sc in next 17 sc] 5 times, 2 sc in next sc, sc in last 16 sc—114 sc.

RND 7: Sc in first 7 sc, [2 sc in next sc, sc in next 18 sc] 5 times, 2 sc in next sc, sc in last 11 sc—120 sc.

Trim 1

RND 1: Sl st in next sc, ch 5 (counts as dc and ch 2), dc in same st, *sk next 3 sc, (dc, ch 2, dc) in next st; rep from * around, sl st in 3rd ch of beg ch-5 to join—30 ch-2 sps.

RND 2: 3 sc in first ch-2 sp, *sc bet next 2 dc, 3 sc in next ch-2 sp; rep from * to last 2 dc, sc bet last 2 dc. Fasten off.

Trim 2

With RS facing and hat upside-down, join B in sc next to m in last even-worked rnd.

RND 1 (JOINING RND): Ch 5 (counts as dc and ch 2), dc in same st, *sk next 2 sc, (dc, ch 2, dc) in next st; rep from * around, sl st in 3rd ch of beg ch-5 to join—26 ch-2 sps.

RND 2: Sl st in first ch-2 sp, ch 8 (counts as tr and ch 3), tr in same sp, [(tr, ch 3, tr) in next ch-2 sp] 25 times, sl st in 5th ch of beg ch-8 to join.

RND 3: 4 sc in first ch-3 sp, *sc bet next 2 tr, 4 sc in next ch-3 sp; rep from * to last 2 tr, sc bet last 2 tr. Fasten off.

TOP OF TRIM 2 AND BOW: With A and leaving a 10" (25.5 cm) tail, ch 26.

With RS facing and hat brim down, join yarn in any sc at beg of trim 2, sc in each st around, ch 26. Leaving a 10" (25.5 cm) tail, fasten off and weave in ends.

Finishing

Tie bow. Lightly iron trims on wool setting through wet cheesecloth. 🍃

NATASHA ROBARGE likes to crochet early in the morning before work. You can see her designs at www.aperfectloop.com.

Finished Size

7" (18 cm) wrist circumference,
8½" (21.5 cm) hand circumference
(buttoned); 7" (18 cm) long.

Yarn

Cascade 220 (100% Peruvian highland
wool; 220 yd [200 m]/3.5 oz [100 g];
(4)): color #9404, 1 skein.

Hook

Size G/6 (4 mm). Adjust hook size if
necessary to obtain correct gauge.

Notions

Yarn needle; eighteen ⅝" (1.5 cm)
vintage-look buttons; matching thread;
sewing needle.

Gauge

16 sts and 15 rows = 4" (10 cm) in st
patt.

----

notes

* Directions written for size S/M. If you
  have larger than average hands, rep
  Rows 4–5 once more after Row 26
  for left mitt. Also, rep Rows 3–4 once
  more after Row 8 for right mitt. This will
  increase the circumference of each mitt
  by ½" (1.3 cm).

* Pay attention to st placement: front
  loop only (flo), back loop only (blo), or
  under both lps (if neither flo nor blo
  is specified, st is worked under both
  loops). The placement of the st creates
  the ribbed texture of the mitts and
  creates more stretch.

* Tch does not count as st.

----

stitch guide

Gauge swatch
Ch 17.

Row 1: Sc in 2nd ch from hook and
each ch across, turn—16 sc.

Row 2: Ch 1 (does not count as st), sc
flo across, turn.

Row 3: Sc blo across.

Rows 4–15: Rep Rows 2–3 six times.
Fasten off.

Betty's Button-Up MITTS
by Brenda K. B. Anderson

It's all about the buttons on Betty's Button-Up Mitts. Use
eighteen matching buttons or a variety of vintage buttons as
I did here. Short-row shaping keeps the wrists snug on these
stylish mitts and stitches through the back loop only create great
stretch and fit.

Left Mitt
Ch 29.

ROW 1: Sc in 2nd ch from hook and in
    each ch across, turn—28 sts.

ROW 2: Ch 1, sc flo across, turn.

ROW 3 (SHORT-ROW): Ch 1, sc blo in
    next 16 sts, sl st blo in next 2 sts,
    turn, sl st flo in next 2 sl sts, sc flo
    in next 16 sts, turn—18 sts worked
    in each direction.

from hook and in each ch across, turn—28 sts.

ROW 2: Ch 1, sc blo across, turn.

ROW 3: Ch 1, sc flo across, turn.

ROWS 4–7: Rep Rows 2–3 two times.

ROW 8 (SHORT-ROW): Sc blo in next 16 sts, sl st blo in next 2 sts, turn, sl st flo in next 2 sl sts, sc flo in next 16 sts, turn—18 sts worked in each direction.

ROWS 9–10: Rep Rows 2–3.

ROW 11: Sc blo in next 8 sts, ch 6, sk next 6 sts (thumbhole made), sc blo in next 14 sts—28 sts.

ROW 12: Rep Row 3.

ROW 13: Rep Row 8.

ROWS 14–17: Rep Rows 2–3 two times.

ROW 18: Rep Row 8.

ROWS 19–22: Rep Rows 2–3 two times.

ROW 23: Rep Row 8.

ROWS 24–25: Rep Rows 2–3.

ROW 26: Rep Row 2. Fasten off.

With RS facing, wrist edge to the right, and finger edge to the left, join yarn with sl st in corner foundation ch.

ROW 27: Sc in first 3 sts, ch 2, working backward (to the right), sl st in first sc of row, working forward, 5 sc in ch-sp just made, sl st around front leg of sc at base of ch (buttonhole made), *sc in next 3 sts, ch 2, sl st in the 3rd sc to the right, 5 sc in ch-sp just made, sl st around front leg of sc at base of ch; rep from * 7 times, sc in last st—9 buttonholes. Turn mitt 90°, 26 sc across finger edge. Fasten off and weave in ends.

Finishing

With needle and thread, sew buttons to long edge opposite buttonholes. 🖋

BRENDA K. B. ANDERSON cooks, crochets, and belly dances. She used to knit, and she probably still would if she could figure out how to let go of her crochet hook. She lives in a little house in Saint Paul with her ridiculously good-looking husband and their hairy baby, Mr. Kittypants.

ROW 4: Ch 1, sc blo across, turn—28 sts.

ROW 5: Ch 1, sc flo across, turn—28 sts.

ROWS 6–7: Rep Rows 4–5.

ROWS 8–12: Rep Rows 3–7.

ROWS 13–15: Rep Rows 3–5.

ROW 16: Ch 1, sc blo in next 8 sts, ch 6, sk next 6 sts (thumbhole made), sc blo in next 14 sts, turn—28 sts.

ROW 17: Rep Row 5.

ROWS 18–22: Rep Rows 3–7.

ROWS 23–26: Rep Rows 4–5 two times.

ROW 27: Ch 1, sc in next 3 sts, ch 2, working backward (to the right), sl st in first sc of row, 5 sc in ch-sp just made, sl st around front leg of sc at base of ch (buttonhole made), *sc in next 3 sts, ch 2, sl st in the 3rd sc to the right, working forward, 5 sc in ch-sp just made, sl st around front leg of sc at base of ch; rep from * 7 times, sc in last st—9 buttonholes. Fasten off.

With RS facing, join yarn in upper right corner of top edge, 26 sc across edge. Fasten off and weave in ends.

Right Mitt

Ch 29.

ROW 1: Turn ch over to work in bottom ridge lp, sc in 2nd ch

Blueberry Trellis HAT
by Anastasia Popova

This clever cloche begins with a cabled brim worked sideways, and then it is worked upward to the crown. A bright button finishes the look. This easy crocheted cable accessory makes a great first cable project and a perfect gift.

Finished Size
18 (19¾, 21½)" (45.5 [50, 54.5] cm) hat circumference. Sample shown is 19¾" (50 cm).

Yarn
NaturallyCaron.com Country (75% microdenier acrylic, 25% merino; 185 yd [170 m]/3 oz [85 g]; (4)): #0013 spruce, 1 (1, 2) skeins.

Hook
Size G/6 (4 mm). Adjust hook size if necessary to obtain correct gauge.

Notions
One 1⅜" (3.5 cm) button, 1 locking or split-ring st marker (m); yarn needle.

Gauge
17 sts and 12 rows in hdc = 4" (10 cm).

----

stitch guide

Gauge swatch
Row 1: Ch 18 (counts as 16 ch and first hdc), hdc in 3rd ch from hook and each ch across, turn—17 hdc.

Row 2: Ch 2, hdc in each st across, turn—17 hdc.

Rep Row 2 ten times. Fasten off.

Pattern

Cable band
ROW 1: (WS) Ch 4 (counts as ch 2 and 1 hdc), hdc in 3rd ch from hook, 2 hdc in last ch, turn—4 hdc.

ROW 2: Ch 2 (counts as hdc), hdc in first 3 sts, 2 hdc in tch, turn—6 hdc.

ROW 3: Ch 2 (counts as hdc), hdc in first 5 sts, 2 hdc in tch, turn—8 hdc.

ROW 4: Ch 2 (does not count as st throughout), hdc in first 3 sts, FPdc (see Glossary) around next 2 sts, hdc in next 3 sts, turn.

ROW 5: Ch 2, hdc in first 2 sts, BPdc (see Glossary) around first post st, hdc in next 2 sts, BPdc around 2nd post st, hdc in last 2 sts, turn.

ROW 6: Ch 2, hdc in first st, FPdc around first post st, hdc in next 4 sts, FPdc around 2nd post st, hdc in last st, turn.

ROW 7: Ch 2, hdc in first st, BPdc around first post st, hdc in next 4 sts, BPdc around 2nd post st, hdc in last st, turn.

ROW 8: Ch 2, hdc in first 2 sts, FPdc around first post st, hdc in next 2 sts, FPdc around 2nd post st, hdc in last 2 sts, turn.

ROW 9: Ch 2, hdc in first 3 sts, BPdc around first post st, BPdc around 2nd post st, hdc in last 3 sts, turn.

ROW 10: Ch 2, hdc in first 3 sts, FPdc around 2nd post st, FPdc around first post st, hdc in last 3 sts, turn.

Rep Rows 5–10 eight (nine, ten) times.

NEXT 2 ROWS: Ch 2, hdc in each st across, turn. Do not turn at the end of last row.

EDGING ROW 1: Ch 1, sc 168 (186, 204) evenly along three edges of cabled band: top, pointy part, and bottom (about 4 sts per 3 rows). Do not turn.

EDGING ROW 2: Ch 1, rev sc (see Glossary) flo in each st across. Do not turn.

Hat

RND 1: (RS) Ch 1 (does not count as st), working behind rev sc, hdc blo in next 77 (84, 91) sc, sc in first hdc to join to work in the rnd, place marker (pm)—77 (84, 91) sts. **NOTE:** Unworked part of cabled band will be overlapped with other end of band and secured with a button in finishing.

RND 2: Hdc in each st around, replacing m in first st of rnd.

Rep last rnd 5 (7, 9) more times, moving m up each rnd.

Crown

RND 1: [Hdc in next 5 sts, hdc2tog (see Glossary)] around—66 (72, 78) sts.

RND 2: [Hdc in next 4 sts, hdc2tog] around—55 (60, 65) sts.

RND 3: Hdc in each st around.

RND 4: [Hdc in next 3 sts, hdc2tog] around—44 (48, 52) sts.

RND 5: [Hdc in next 2 sts, hdc2tog] around—33 (36, 39) sts.

RND 6: Hdc in each st around.

RND 7: [Hdc in next st, hdc2tog] around—22 (24, 26) sts.

RND 8: Hdc2tog around—11 (12, 13) sts.

Fasten off, leaving 5" (12.5 cm) tail.

Finishing

With yarn needle, thread yarn tail through top of rem lps and pull tight to close. Secure and weave in end.

Lay free end of cabled band on top of other side of band. With yarn needle and piece of yarn 10" (25.5 cm) long, sew button at beg of first cable. 🌀

ANASTASIA POPOVA is the founder of CrochetNJ.com, a New Jersey community of crocheters. She enjoys designing and teaching others to crochet. She blogs at www.anastasiapopova.com.

Cable Band

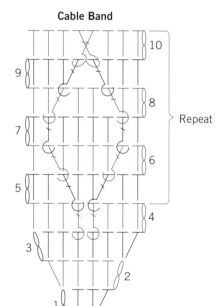

Stitch Key

⬯ = chain (ch)

| = half double crochet (hdc)

⊥ = Front Post double crochet (FPdc)

⊥ = Back Post double crochet (BPdc)

Finished Size

About 9" (23 cm) diameter.

Yarn

Red Heart Soft Solids (100% acrylic; 256 yd [234 m]/5 oz [140 g]; (4)): #9925 really red (MC), 1 skein. Red Heart Designer Sport (100% acrylic; 279 yd [255 m]/3 oz [85 g]; (3)): #3515 lagoon (CC), 1 skein.

Hook

Sizes H/8 (5 mm), G/6 (4 mm). Adjust hook size if necessary to obtain correct gauge.

Notions

16 colors of scrap yarn (3 pieces of each color, each about 4" [10 cm] long), 6¼" (16 cm) purse frame with handle (sew on style); 6 st markers (m; 1 of these markers should be in a contrasting color); yarn needle; sewing needle and thread (matching MC).

Gauge

14 sts and 8 rows = 4" (10 cm) in hdc blo on larger hook with MC. Work through Rnd 9 of lining patt with CC and smaller hook. Circle should measure 4" (10 cm) diameter.

---

notes

* Tch does not count as st.

* Outer bag is worked in one long wavy strip, then twisted and sewn tog to form a pouch. (Outer bag is assembled inside out, and after seams are sewn, turned RS out.) The short ends of the strip become the opening at the top of the pouch and are sewn to the outside of the purse frame. Lining is constructed in the rnd, inc from center outward in a continuous spiral (do not join rnds), then sts are skipped for opening, then dec to center of other side of lining. It is then sewn to the inside of the purse frame around the opening.

Pattern

Outer bag

With MC and larger hook, ch 130.

ROW 1: Hdc in 3rd ch from hook, working in bottom ridge lp, hdc in next 7 sts, sc in next 4 sts, sl st in next 4 sts, [sl st in next 4 sts, sc in next 4 sts, hdc in next 16 sts, sc in next 4 sts, sl st in next 4 sts] 3 times, sl st in next 4 sts, sc in next 4 sts, hdc in next 8 sts, turn—128 sts.

Twist Bag

by Brenda K. B. Anderson

This innovative bag is perfect for a night on the town. With a little clever seaming, a long wavy strip twists into a cute little crocheted bag. A crocheted lining gives it heft plus a jazzy contrast color. Add a purse frame that reflects your own personality.

ROW 2: Hdc in 3rd ch from hook, working in blo (see Glossary) throughout, hdc in next 7 sts, sc in next 4 sts, sl st in next 4 sts, [sl st in next 4 sts, sc in next 4 sts, hdc in next 16 sts, sc in next 4 sts, sl st in next 4 sts] 3 times, sl st in next 4 sts, sc in next 4 sts, hdc in next 8 sts, turn—128 sts.

ROWS 3–14: Rep Row 2. Fasten off.

Bag lining

RND 1: With smaller hook and CC make an adjustable ring (see Glossary), 6 sc in ring, pull beg yarn tail to close lp—6 sts.

RND 2: 2 sc in each of the next 6 sts—12 sts.

RND 3: [Sc in next st, 2 sc in next st (inc made)] 6 times—18 sts.

RND 4: [2 sc in next st, sc in next 2 sts] 6 times—24 sts.

RND 5: [Sc in next 2 sts, 2 sc in next st, sc in next st] 6 times—30 sts.

RND 6: [Sc in next 4 sts, 2 sc in next st] 6 times—36 sts.

RND 7: [Sc in next 2 sts, 2 sc in next st, sc in next 3 sts, place marker (pm; use contrasting m in last st of rnd)] 6 times—42 sts, and 6 m placed.

RNDS 8–18: Sc around making 1 inc bet each set of m (make inc in different place each rnd)—108 sts at end of Rnd 18, 18 sts bet each set of m.

RNDS 19–23: Sc around—108 sts.

RND 24: Ch 30, sk next 30 sts (for opening), sc in rem 78 sts—108 sts.

RNDS 25–28: Sc around—108 sts.

RND 29: [Sc in next 16 sts, sc2tog (dec made)] 6 times—102 sts.

RNDS 30–45: Sc around, making 1 dec bet each set of m—6 sts at end of Rnd 45.

Fasten off. Weave in ends.

Assembly

MAKE A COLOR KEY AS FOLL: On a piece of paper write down letters of the alphabet from A–P; staple or tape a different color 4" (10 cm) piece of yarn next to each letter.

TO MARK A ST: Insert hook into st, lay center of 4" (10 cm) piece of yarn over hook, and pull up lp, yo with both yarn ends, and draw through lp on hook.

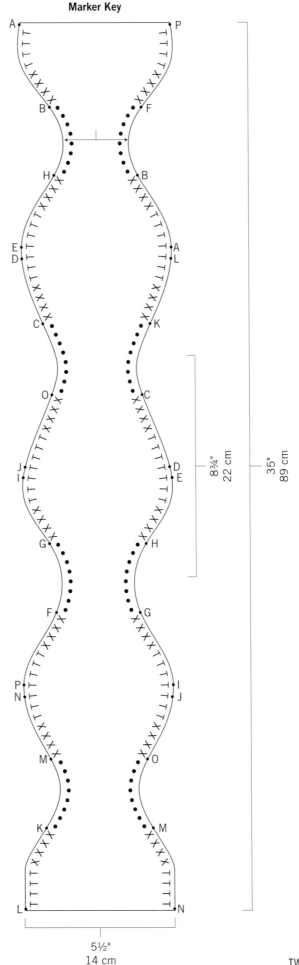

Marker Key

8¾"
22 cm

35"
89 cm

5½"
14 cm

Figure 1

Top edge #1

A • A

B • B

C • C

D E

D • E

Stitch A to B
and C to D

D

E

Top edge #2

ASSEMBLE OUTER BAG

NOTE: Either side of outer bag is RS. Sections of sl st are at center of twists and sections of hdc are along outer circumference of bag when assembled. Remove scraps of yarn as you sew bag tog. Use a woven seam (see Glossary), worked through flo.

1. Mark outer bag with scrap yarn, according to key.

2. Lay strip out on table or floor to match orientation in diagram. Matching A to A and B to B, with MC and yarn needle, sew from point A to point B (see **figure 1**). Match points C to C, D to D, and E to E. Sew from point C to point E.

3. Fold top section to the left like turning a page (see **figure 2**).

4. Take top edge #2 and thread through gap near point B, twisting strip once counterclockwise. Pull through until F matches with F, and H matches with H. Match G up with G (around the B/F sl st section). Sew from H to D. Sew from G through I and J (see **figures 3a** and **3b**).

5. Flip piece over like turning a page (see **figure 4**). Feed top edge #2 through gap near point C, twisting once counterclockwise to match K to K, and L to L. Sew from K to L. Match M to M, N to N, O to O and P to P. Sew from M to N and from O to J and P to F.

Weave in ends. Turn RS out.

Opening edge

With MC and larger hook, work 3 sc for every 2 hdc row-ends and 1 sc in corner/point where opening starts on each side—21 sc in each side of opening, and 1 sc bet each side, 44 sc total around opening. Make sure this opening will be the same size as purse frame opening. If too small for frame, stretch edge more and add extra sc as needed. If too big, make fewer sc so as to not stretch edge. Sl st in first sc made and fasten off. Weave in ends.

Place outer bag edge on the outside of the edges of purse frame. With sewing needle and thread, sew opening of outer bag to holes in purse frame. Place bag lining inside outer bag, matching opening with inside of purse frame. push lining into place using both fists inside bag, pulling away from each other. Sew top opening in place through outer bag and through holes in frame. Thread should match MC, but it should disappear into the lining and won't be noticeable. 🍃

BRENDA K. B. ANDERSON cooks, crochets, and belly dances. She used to knit, and she probably still would if she could figure out how to let go of her crochet hook. She lives in a little house in Saint Paul with her ridiculously good-looking husband and their hairy baby, Mr. Kittypants.

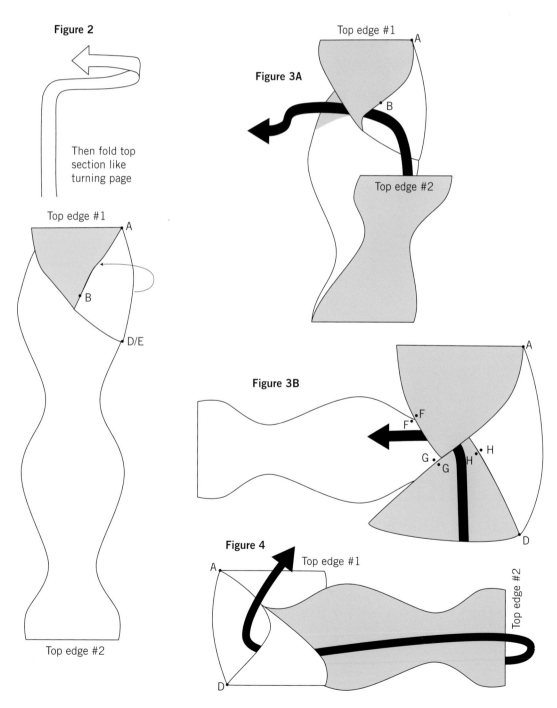

Figure 2

Then fold top section like turning page

Top edge #1

A

B

D/E

Top edge #2

Figure 3A

Top edge #1

A

B

Top edge #2

Figure 3B

A

F
F

G
G

H
H

D

Figure 4

A

Top edge #1

D

Top edge #2

Digory Mittens

by Brenda K. B. Anderson

Cables interlock against a slip-stitch background on these überwarm, deliciously comfortable mittens. The body of each mitten is worked flat from the top down in turned rows of slip stitch through the back loop only. A variety of sizes makes these thick mittens a great gift.

Finished Size
7½ (8½, 9¼)" (19 [21.5, 23.5] cm) palm circumference above thumb and 9" (9¾, 10½)" (23 [25, 26.5] cm) long, to fit woman's small/medium (woman's medium/large, man's small/medium). Mittens shown measure 8½" (21.5 cm) in circumference.

Yarn
Caron Sheep(ish), (70% acrylic, 30% wool; 167 yd [153 m]/3 oz [85 g]; (4)): #0011 taupe(ish), 2 (2, 3) balls.

Hook
Size I/9 (5.5 mm). Adjust hook size if necessary to obtain correct gauge.

Notions
St markers (m); yarn needle.

Gauge
19 sts and 32 rows = 4" (10 cm) in sl st blo.

notes

✸ Mittens are worked flat from the top down in turned rows of sl st blo (see Glossary). Thumb is worked in the rnd after main part of mitten is complete.

✸ These mittens are fairly thick, and the inner circumference is smaller than the outer circumference. The mittens will stretch lengthwise but not very much widthwise.

✸ The diamond cables are made from a combination of FPtr, FPdtr, and FPdc (see Glossary) sts on a background of sl st blo.

✸ It may be helpful to pm in first and last st of cable panel and move m up each row.

stitch guide

Slip-stitch two together back lp only (slst2tog blo)
Insert hook in the back lp of the next st then through the back lp of the foll st, yo, and pull through all 3 lps on hook.

Slip-stitch ridges
When working stitch in a sl st ridge, you are working into the front lp of one row and the back lp of the next row at the same time. This technique is used to start each one of the three cables. If you have trouble counting ridges, stretch out the mitten lengthwise a bit and the ridges will become much clearer. Ridges are counted starting from the tip of the mitten and moving toward the wrist.

Right Mitten

ROW 1: (RS) Make an adjustable ring (see Glossary), 6 (7, 7) sc into ring, turn (do not join)—6 (7, 7) sc. Pull tail to tighten ring.

ROW 2: (WS) Ch 1, 2 sc in each sc across, turn—12 (14, 14) sc.

ROW 3: Ch 1, [sc in next st, 2 sc in next st] 6 (7, 7) times, turn—18 (21, 21) sc. With RS facing, mark the post of the 12th and 14th (15th and 17th, 15th and 17th) sts with st markers (m). Do not remove m until Row 19.

ROW 4: Ch 1, [sl st blo (see Glossary) in next 2 sts, 2 sl st blo in next st] 6 (7, 7) times, turn—24 (28, 28) sl sts.

ROW 5: Ch 1, sl st blo across, turn.

ROW 6: Ch 1, [2 sl st blo in next st, sl st blo in next 3 (3, 2) sts] 6 (6, 8) times, sl st blo in next 0 (4, 4) sts, turn—30 (34, 36) sts.

ROW 7: Ch 1, sl st blo across, turn.

ROW 8: Ch 1, 2 sl st blo in next 0 (0, 1) sts, [sl st blo in next 4 sts, 2 sl st blo in next st] 6 (6, 7) times, sl st blo in next 0 (4, 0) sts, turn—36 (40, 44) sts.

ROW 9: Ch 1, sl st blo in next 22 (26, 30) sts, working in the first ridge of sl sts made (this ridge was created by the front lp of Row 3, and the back lp of Row 4), tr in 2nd marked st (remove m), tr in next st to the left (still working in the same sl st ridge), sk next 2 sts on working row, sl st blo in next st, working in same sl st ridge as before, count 2 sts to the right of the first tr made, tr in this marked stitch (remove marker), tr in next st to the left, sk next 2 sts on working row, sl st blo in last 9 sts, turn.

ROWS 10–14: Ch 1, sl st blo across, turn.

On Row 11, mark the posts of the 18th, 20th, 29th, and 31st sts for size 8½" (21.5 cm); 22nd, 24th, 33rd, and 35th sts for size 9¼" (23.5 cm); 26th, 28th, 37th, and 39th sts for size 10" (25.5 cm).

ROW 15: Ch 1, sl st blo in next 20 (24, 28) sts, FPtr around next 2 tr from 6 rows below, sk next 2 sts on working row, sl st blo in next 5 sts, FPtr around next 2 tr from 6 rows below, sk next 2 sts on working row, sl st blo in last 7 sts, turn.

ROWS 16–18: Rep Row 10.

ROW 19: Ch 1, sl st blo in next 16 (20, 24) sts, *working in the 5th sl st ridge, tr in 2nd marked st from Row 11 (remove m), tr in next st to the left (still working in the same sl st ridge), sk next 2 sts on working row, sl st blo in next st, working in same sl st ridge as before, tr in first marked st from Row 11, tr in foll st**, sk next 2 sts on current row, sl st in next 7 sts; rep from * to ** for next pair of markers from Row 11, sk next sts on current row, sl st blo in last 3 sts, turn.

ROW 20: Rep Row 10.

ROW 21: Ch 1, sl st blo in first 14 (18, 22) sts, work Row 1 of cable panel over next 21 sts, sl st blo in 1 st, turn.

ROW 22: Ch 1, sl st blo in 1 st, work Row 2 of cable panel over next 21 sts, sl st blo in last 14 (18, 22) sts, turn.

ROWS 23–39 (23–45, 23–51): Work even in patt as set.

Make thumbhole

ROW 40 (46, 52): Ch 1, sl st blo in first 20 (22, 24) sts, ch 10 (12, 14), sk next 4 sts, sl st blo in last 12 (14, 16) sts, turn—42 (48, 54) sts.

ROWS 41–49 (46–55, 53–61): Work even, keeping cable panel as set and working thumb sts in sl st blo.

Shape thumb gusset

ROW 50 (56, 62): Ch 1, sl st blo in first 20 (22, 24) sts, slst2tog blo (mark this st), sl st blo in next 6 (8, 10) sts, slst2tog blo (mark this st), sl st blo in last 12 (14, 16) sts, turn—40 (46, 52) sts.

ROW 51 (57, 63): Work even in patt.

ROW 52 (58, 64): Ch 1, sl st blo in first 19 (21, 23) sts, slst2tog blo, sl st blo in next 6 (8, 10) sts, slst2tog blo, sl st blo in last 11 (13, 15) sts, turn—38 (44, 50) sts.

ROW 53 (59, 65): Work even in patt.

ROW 54 (60, 66): Ch 1, sl st blo in first 18 (20, 22) sts, slst2tog blo, sl st blo in next 6 (8, 10) sts, slst2tog blo, sl st blo in last 10 (12, 14) sts, turn—36 (42, 48) sts.

ROW 55 (61, 67): Work even in patt.

ROW 56 (62, 68): Ch 1, sl st blo in first 20 (21, 24) sts, slst2tog blo, sl st blo in next 2 (2, 4) sts, slst2tog blo, sl st blo in last 10 (13, 16) sts, turn—34 (40, 46) sts.

ROW 57 (63, 69): Work even in patt.

Size 7½" (19 cm) only

ROW 58: Ch 1, sl st blo in first 19 sts, slst2tog blo, sl st blo in next 2 sts, slst2tog blo, sl st blo in last 9 sts, turn—32 sts.

ROWS 59–66: Work even in patt.

ROW 67: Ch 1, sl st blo in first 12 sts, [FPtr around next 2 FPtr from 6 rows below, sk next 2 sts on current row, sl st blo in next st] twice, [FPdc around next 2 FPdtr from 4 rows below, sk next 2 sts on current row, sl st blo in next st] twice, [FPtr around next 2 FPtr from 6 rows below, sk next 2 sts on current row, sl st blo in next st] twice, sl st blo in last 2 sts, turn.

ROWS 68–71: Ch 1, sl st blo across, turn. Fasten off, leaving a long tail.

Size 8½" (21.5 cm) only

ROW 64: Ch 1, sl st blo in first 20 sts, [slst2tog blo] 2 times, sl st blo in next 2 sts, [slst2tog blo] 2 times, sl st blo in last 12 sts—36 sts.

ROWS 65–72: Work even in patt.

ROW 73: Ch 1, sl st blo in first 16 sts, *sk next 2 FPtr from 6 rows below, FPdtr around next 2 FPtr, sk next 2 sts on current row, sl st blo in next st, FPdtr around each of the 2 skipped FPtr, sk next 2 sts on current row**, sl st blo in next st, [FPdc around next 2 FPtr from 4 rows below, sk next 2 sts on current row, sl st blo in next st] twice; rep from * to **, sl st blo in last 3 sts, turn.

ROWS 74–77: Ch 1, sl st blo across, turn. Fasten off, leaving a long tail.

Size 9¼" (23.5 cm) only

ROW 70: Ch 1, sl st blo in first 23 sts, [slst2tog blo] 2 times, sl st blo in next 2 sts, [slst2tog blo] 2 times, sl st blo in last 15 sts—42 sts.

ROW 71: Work even in patt.

ROW 72: Ch 1, sl st blo in first 22 sts, slst2tog blo, sl st blo in next 2 sts, slst2tog blo, sl st blo in last 14 sts, turn—40 sts.

ROW 73: Ch 1, sl st blo in first 20 sts, *sk next 2 FPtr from 6 rows below, FPdtr around next 2 FPtr, sk next 2 sts on current row, sl st blo in next st, FPdtr around each of the 2 skipped FPtr, sk next sts on current row**, sl st blo in next st, [FPdc around next 2 FPtr from 4 rows below, sk next 2 sts on current row, sl st blo in next st] twice; rep from * to **, sl st blo in last 3 sts, turn.

ROWS 74–83: Ch 1, sl st blo across, turn. Fasten off, leaving a long tail.

Left Mitten

ROWS 1–3: Rep as for Right Mitten.

With RS facing, mark the post of the 6th and 8th sts with stitch markers. Do not remove these markers until Row 19.

ROWS 4–8: Work as for Right Mitten.

ROW 9: Ch 1, sl st blo in next 9 sts, working in the first ridge of sl sts made (this ridge was created by the front lp of Row 3, and the back lp of Row 4), tr in 2nd marked st (remove m), tr in next st to the left (still working in the same sl st ridge), sk next 2 sts on working row, sl st blo in next st, working in same sl st ridge as before, count 2 sts to the right of the first tr made, tr in this marked stitch (remove marker), tr in next st to the left, sk next 2 sts on working row, sl st blo in last 22 (26, 30) sts, turn—36 (40, 44) sts.

ROWS 10–14: Ch 1, sl st blo across, turn.

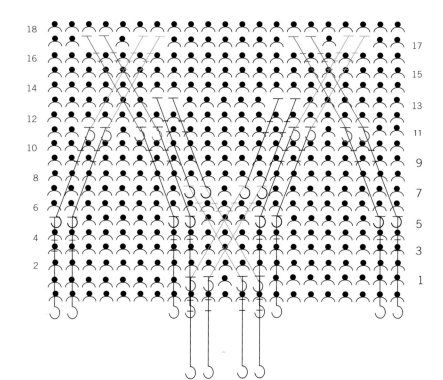

Stitch Key

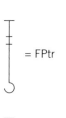

$\mathbf{\curvearrowright}$ = sl st blo

= FPtr

= FPdtr

On Row 11, mark the posts of the 5th, 7th, 16th, and 18th sts.

ROW 15: Ch 1, sl st blo in next 7 sts, FPtr around next 2 tr from 6 rows below, sk next 2 sts on working row, sl st blo in next 5 sts, FPtr around next 2 tr from 6 rows below, sk next 2 sts on working row, sl st blo in last 20 (24, 28) sts, turn.

ROWS 16–18: Rep Row 10.

ROW 19: Ch 1, sl st blo in next 3 sts, *working in the 5th sl st ridge, tr in 2nd marked st from Row 11 (remove m), tr in next st to the left (still working in the same sl st ridge), sk next 2 sts on working row, sl st blo in next st, working in same sl st ridge as before, tr in first marked st from Row 11, tr in foll st**, sk next 2 sts on current row, sl st in next 7 sts; rep from * to ** for next pair of markers from Row 11, sk next sts on current row, sl st blo in last 16 (20, 24) sts, turn.

ROW 20: Rep Row 10.

ROW 21: Ch 1, sl st blo in first st, work Row 1 of cable panel over next 21 sts, sl st blo in 14 (18, 22) sts, turn.

ROW 22: Ch 1, sl st blo in 14 (18, 22) sts, work Row 2 of cable panel over next 21 sts, sl st blo in last st, turn.

ROWS 23–39 (23–45, 23–51): Work even in patt as set.

Make thumbhole

ROW 40 (46, 52): Ch 1, sl st blo in first 12 (14, 16) sts, ch 10 (12, 14), sk next 4 sts, sl st blo in last 20 (22, 24) sts, turn—42 (48, 54) sts.

ROWS 41–49 (46–55, 53–61): Work even, keeping cable panel as set and working thumb sts in sl st blo.

Shape thumb gusset

ROW 50 (56, 62): Ch 1, sl st blo in first 12 (14, 16) sts, slst2tog blo (mark this st), sl st blo in next 6 (8, 10) sts, slst2tog blo (mark this st), sl st blo in last 20 (22, 24) sts, turn—40 (46, 52) sts.

ROW 51 (57, 63): Work even in patt.

ROW 52 (58, 64): Ch 1, sl st blo in first 11 (13, 15) sts, slst2tog blo, sl st blo in next 6 (8, 10) sts, slst2tog blo, sl st blo in last 19 (21, 23) sts, turn—38 (44, 50) sts.

ROW 53 (59, 65): Work even in patt.

ROW 54 (60, 66): Ch 1, sl st blo in first 10 (12, 14) sts, slst2tog blo, sl st blo in next 6 (8, 10) sts, slst2tog blo, sl st blo in last 18 (20, 22) sts, turn—36 (42, 48) sts.

ROW 55 (61, 67): Work even in patt.

ROW 56 (62, 68): Ch 1, sl st blo in first 10 (13, 16) sts, slst2tog blo, sl st blo in next 2 (2, 4) sts, slst2tog blo, sl st blo in last 20 (21, 24) sts, turn—34 (40, 46) sts.

ROW 57 (63, 69): Work even in patt.

Size 7½" (19 cm) only

ROW 58: Ch 1, sl st blo in first 9 sts, slst2tog blo, sl st blo in next 2 sts, slst2tog blo, sl st blo in last 19 sts, turn—32 sts.

ROWS 59–66: Work even in patt.

ROW 67: Ch 1, sl st blo in first 2 sts, [FPtr around next 2 FPtr from 6 rows below, sk next 2 sts on current row, sl st blo in next st] twice, [FPdc around next 2 FPdtr from 4 rows below, sk next 2 sts on current row, sl st blo in next st] twice, [FPtr around next 2 FPtr from 6 rows below, sk next 2 sts on current row, sl st blo in next st] twice, sl st blo in last 12 sts, turn.

ROWS 68–71: Ch 1, sl st blo across, turn. Fasten off, leaving a long tail.

Size 8½" (21.5 cm) only

ROW 64: Ch 1, sl st blo in first 12 sts, [slst2tog blo] 2 times, sl st blo in next 2 sts, [slst2tog blo] 2 times, sl st blo in last 20 sts—36 sts.

ROWS 65–72: Work even in patt.

ROW 73: Ch 1, sl st blo in first 3 sts, *sk next 2 FPtr from 6 rows below, FPdtr around next 2 FPtr, sk next 2 sts on current row, sl st blo in next st, FPdtr around each of the 2 skipped FPtr, sk next 2 sts on current row**, sl st blo in next st, [FPdc around next 2 FPtr from 4 rows below, sk next 2 sts on current row, sl st blo in next st] twice; rep from * to **, sl st blo in last 16 sts, turn.

ROWS 74–77: Ch 1, sl st blo across, turn. Fasten off, leaving a long tail.

Size 9¼" (23.5 cm) only

ROW 70: Ch 1, sl st blo in first 15 sts, [slst2tog blo] 2 times, sl st blo in next 2 sts, [slst2tog blo] 2 times, sl st blo in last 23 sts—42 sts.

ROW 71: Work even in patt.

ROW 72: Ch 1, sl st blo in first 14 sts, slst2tog blo, sl st blo in next 2 sts, slst2tog blo, sl st blo in last 22 sts, turn—40 sts.

ROW 73: Ch 1, sl st blo in first 3 sts, *sk next 2 FPtr from 6 rows below, FPdtr around next 2 FPtr, sk next 2 sts on current row, sl st blo in next st, FPdtr around each of the 2 skipped FPtr, sk next sts on current row**, sl st blo in next st, [FPdc around next 2 FPtr from 4 rows below, sk next 2 sts on current row, sl st blo in next st] twice; rep from * to **, sl st blo in last 20 sts, turn.

ROWS 74–83: Ch 1, sl st blo across, turn. Fasten off, leaving a long tail.

Thumb

With RS facing, join yarn in any st of thumbhole.

RND 1: Work 14 (16, 18) sl st blo evenly around thumbhole. Do not join.

Work in sl st blo for 13 (15, 17) more rnds, or to desired length.

NEXT RND: Slst2tog blo 7 (8, 9) times—7 (8, 9) sts.

Fasten off, run yarn tail through rem 7 (8, 9) sts and pull tight. Weave in ends securely.

Finishing

With yarn needle and long tail, sew side seams of mittens using mattress stitch. Weave in ends. Block. 🖊

BRENDA K. B. ANDERSON cooks, crochets, and belly dances. She used to knit, and she probably still would if she could figure out how to let go of her crochet hook. She lives in a little house in Saint Paul with her ridiculously good-looking husband and their hairy baby, Mr. Kittypants.

Snowdrops SCARF
by Doris Chan

This simple lace scarf features a scrollwork border taken from a book of charted Celtic designs. Charts of this nature are often used as templates for colorwork, but they translate perfectly into the positive- and negative-space aspects of filet crochet. Quickly and easily crocheted in an exploded gauge using creamy-soft cashmere-blend yarn, this scarf makes for a luxurious accessory and a handsome gift.

Finished Size
8" × 64" (20.5 × 162.5 cm) blocked.

Yarn
Lion Brand Cashmere Blend (72% merino wool, 14% cashmere, 14% nylon; 84 yd [77 m]/1.5 oz [40 g]; (4)): #105 light blue, 4 balls.

Hook
Size J/10 (6 mm) crochet hook. Adjust hook size if necessary to obtain gauge.

Gauge
13 sts = 4" (10 cm) and 4 rows = 3" (7.5 cm) unblocked in filet patt. Gauge is not crucial for project.

---

notes

* Scarf measures 8½" (21.5 cm) wide and 60" (152.5 cm) long unblocked. This is a 3-st filet that uses 2 sts to fill a block and 2 ch for an empty block. The chart is RS facing. Each square represents one block. Read chart in reverse for WS rows. Scarf has no obvious RS or WS.

---

stitch guide

Extended dc (edc)
Yo, insert hook in next st, yo and pull up lp (3 lps on hook), yo and pull through 1 lp, [yo and pull through 2 lps] 2 times.

Scarf

ROW 1: Fdc (see Glossary) 28 (counts as 1 edge st and nine 3-st blocks), turn—9 filled blocks.

ROW 2: Ch 3, sk first dc, edc (see Stitch Guide) in next 3 dc (filled block), [ch 2, sk next 2 dc, edc in next dc] 7 times (7 empty blocks), edc in next 2 dc, edc in top of tch (filled block), turn—1 edge st, 9 blocks.

ROW 3: Ch 3, sk first edc, edc in next 3 edc, [ch 2, sk next ch-2 sp, edc in next edc] 3 times, 2 edc in next ch-2 sp, edc in next edc, [ch 2, sk next ch-2 sp, edc in next edc] 3 times, edc in next 2 edc, edc in top of tch, turn.

ROW 4: Ch 3, sk first edc, edc in next 3 edc, [ch 2, sk next ch-2 sp, edc in next edc] 2 times, 2 edc in next ch-2 sp, edc in next edc, edc in next 3 edc, 2 edc in next ch-2 sp, edc in next edc, [ch 2, sk next ch-2 sp, edc in next edc] 2 times, edc in next 2 edc, edc in top of tch, turn.

ROWS 5–17: Work Rows 5–17 of Filet chart (see Notes).

Filet

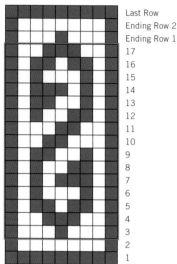

Last Row
Ending Row 2
Ending Row 1
17
16
15
14
13
12
11
10
9
8
7
6
5
4
3
2
1

Rep Rows 3–17 for patt

ROWS 18–77: Rep Rows 3–17 of chart 4 more times (or to desired length).

ROWS 78–80: Work last 3 rows of chart.

Fasten off and weave in loose ends. Block to measurements. Avoid stretching scarf too much when damp. Gently flatten to measurements and allow to dry completely. **NOTE:** Blocking opens and squares up the filet and makes the pattern really pop. 🍂

Exploded filet crochet is one of the ways **DORIS CHAN** explores her love for lace and lacy patterns, which she shares in her two books, *Amazing Crochet Lace, Everyday Crochet,* and *Crochet Lace Innovations* (Potter Craft, 2006, 2007, and 2010 respectively). Visit her at dorischancrochet.com for more musings from one who crochets every day.

Candy CLOCHE
by Linda Permann

In the first row of this hat, a row of chains is cleverly transformed into the pretty confection that is the star stitch. Alternating rows of star stitch and single crochet form the brim of this ladylike cloche, and simple single crochet with decreases shape the top of the hat. The flattering gentle curves will keep your head warm with style through the winter. The cloche is accented with colorful buttons, but you could also adorn it with a flower, bow, or whatever suits your style.

Finished Size

26" (66 cm) circumference at brim to fit average woman's head.

Yarn

Valley Yarns Berkshire Bulky (85% wool, 15% alpaca; 108 yd [100 m]/3.5 oz [100 g]; (**5**)): #26 periwinkle, 2 balls. Yarn distributed by WEBS.

Hook

Size K/10½ (6.5 mm) hook. Adjust hook size if necessary to obtain correct gauge.

Notions

Stitch marker (m); yarn needle; assorted colorful buttons; needle and thread.

Gauge

12 sts and 4 rows = 4" (10 cm) in sc.

notes

* Hat is worked from the bottom up.

* Top of closing lp of each star st is st where subsequent row of sc is worked.

* Top of hat may have a slight bump. Block hat to smooth bump.

stitch guide

Star st

Insert hook in first st, yo and pull up lp, [insert hook in next st, yo and pull up lp] 4 times (6 lps on hook), yo and draw through all 6 lps on hook, ch 1 to close st, *insert hook in closing lp of last star, yo and pull up lp, insert hook in st where last star finished, yo and pull up lp, [insert hook in next st, yo and pull up lp] 3 times, yo and draw through all 6 lps on hook, ch 1 to close st; rep from * across.

Hat

Ch 107, sc in first ch to form ring being careful not to twist ch.

RND 1: Ch 1, star st (see Stitch Guide) across foundation row, sl st in first star to join—35 star sts.

RND 2: Ch 1, 3 sc in each star st to last star st, 4 sc in last star st, sl st in first sc to join—106 sc.

RND 3: Ch 1, star st across, sl st in first star st to join—35 star sts.

RND 4: Ch 1, *3 sc in next 2 star sts, 2 sc in next star st; rep from * 9 times, 3 sc in next 5 star sts, sl st in first sc to join—95 sc.

RND 5: Ch 1, star st across, sl st in first star st to join—31 star sts.

RND 6: *3 sc in next 4 star sts, 2 sc in next star st; rep from * 4 times, 3 sc in next 2 star sts, 2 sc in each of last 4 star sts, place marker (pm) in last st—84 sc.

NOTE: Remainder of hat is worked in a spiral (instead of joining at the end of each rnd). Move m up to last st of each rnd.

RND 7: Sc around—84 sc.

RND 8: *Sc in next 5 sc, sc2tog (see Glossary); rep from * around—72 sc.

RND 9: Sc around—72 sc.

RND 10: *Sc in next 4 sc, sc2tog; rep from * around—60 sc.

RND 11: Sc around—60 sc.

RNDS 12–16: Rep Rnd 11—60 sc.

RND 17: *Sc in next 8 sc, sc2tog; rep from * around—54 sc.

RND 18: Sc around—54 sc.

RND 19: *Sc in next 7 sc, sc2tog; rep from * around—48 sc.

RND 20: *Sc in next 6 sc, sc2tog; rep from * around—42 sc.

RND 21: *Sc in next 5 sc, sc2tog; rep from * around—36 sc.

RND 22: *Sc in next 4 sc, sc2tog; rep from * around—30 sc.

RND 23: *Sc in next 3 sc, sc2tog; rep from * around—24 sc.

RND 24: *Sc in next 6 sc, sc2tog; rep from * around—21 sc.

RND 25: *Sc in next 5 sc, sc2tog; rep from * around—18 sc.

RND 26: *Sc in next 4 sc, sc2tog; rep from * around—15 sc.

RND 27: *Sc in next 3 sc, sc2tog; rep from * around—12 sc.

RND 28: *Sc in next 2 sc, sc2tog; rep from * around—9 sc.

Cut yarn, leaving a 12" (30.5 cm) tail. Using tail end, draw a lp through each of 9 sts of last rnd, moving lps to a safety pin if it becomes difficult to keep all 9 sts on hook. With yarn needle, thread tail through all 9 lps and pull taut (removing safety pin, if using). Fasten off and weave in loose ends. Sew buttons to front side edge of cloche. ✍

LINDA PERMANN is a crochet and craft designer who lives in Bozeman, Montana. She is the author of *Crochet Adorned: Reinvent Your Wardrobe with Crocheted Accents, Embellishments, and Trims* (Potter Craft, 2009). See more of her work at www.lindamade.com.

Granny BAG

by Mags Kandis

Granny squares have been in my life for as long as I can remember. They were probably the first thing I mastered as a fledging crafty-gal. I believe that a granny-square throw is the ultimate gift, but a project of that size may be too much of a commitment. This bag condenses all the joy of a crazy patchwork throw into one compact, heartfelt package. When lining this type of bag, I like to add a little patch with a word of inspiration—"smile" in this case.

Finished Size
About 13" (33 cm) wide and 14½" (37 cm) long, after felting and excluding handles.

Yarn
Sportweight (#2 Fine).

Shown here: Brown Sheep Nature Spun Sport (100% wool; 184 yd [168 m]/50 g): #225S brick road (A), #107S silver sage (B), #N17S French clay (C), #N80S mountain purple (D), #117S winter blue (E), #104S Grecian olive (F), #308S sunburst gold (G), #880S charcoal (H), #209 wood moss (I), #146S pomegranate (J), and #N18 plum line (K), 1 ball each.

Hook
Size G/6 (4 mm). Adjust hook size if necessary to obtain the correct gauge.

Notions
Tapestry needle; set of two rattan handles measuring 6" (15 cm) high and 7½" (19 cm) wide (handles shown here are style hr1 from tallpoppycraft.com); straight pins; about ½ yard (46 cm) lining fabric; matching thread. Makings for patch (optional): small scrap of fabric; iron-on adhesive; contrast thread; fabric ink pad in black; alphabet stamps.

Gauge
Large square measures 5½" (14 cm) square before felting and 4" (10 cm) square after felting.

- -
stitch guide
- -

Large Square
Ch 5, sl st in first ch to form ring.

Rnd 1: Ch 2 (counts as 1 dc), 2dc in ring, ch 2, [3dc in ring, ch 2] 3 times, sl st in second ch of beg ch-2 to join—four ch-2 spaces.

Rnd 2: Ch 4 (counts as dc and ch 2), *(3dc, ch 2, 3dc) in next ch-2 sp, ch 2; rep from * 2 more times, 3dc, 2 ch, 2dc into last ch-2 sp, sl st in second ch of beg ch-4 to join—8 ch-2 sps.

Rnd 3: Ch 2 (counts as 1dc), 2dc in same ch-2 sp, ch 2, (3dc, ch 2, 3dc) in next ch-2 sp, ch 2, *3dc in next ch-2 sp, ch 2, (3 dc, 2 ch, 3dc) in the next ch-2 sp, ch 2; rep from * 2 more times, sl st in second ch of beg ch-2 to join—12 ch-2 sps.

Rnd 4: Ch 4 (counts as dc and ch 2), 3dc in next ch-2 sp, ch 2, (3dc, ch 2, 3dc) in next ch-2 sp, ch 2, *[3dc in next ch-2 sp, ch 2] 2 times, (3dc, ch 2, 3dc) in next ch-2 sp, ch 2; rep from * 2 more times, 2dc into the last ch-2 sp, sl st in second ch of beg ch-4 to join—16 ch-2 sps.

Rnd 5: Ch 2 (counts as 1 dc), 2 dc in same ch-2 sp, ch 2, 3 dc in next ch-2 sp, ch 2, (3 dc, 2 ch, 3dc) in next ch-2 sp, ch 2, *[3 dc in next ch-2 sp, ch 2] 3 times, (3 dc, ch 2, 3dc) in next ch-2 sp, ch 2; rep from * 2 more times, 3 dc into the last ch-2 sp, ch 2, sl st in second ch of beg ch-2 to join—20 ch-2 sps.

Rnd 6: Ch 4 (counts as dc and ch 2), [3dc in next ch-2 sp, ch 2] 2 times, (3dc, ch 2, 3dc) in next ch-2 sp, ch 2, *[3dc in next ch-2 sp, ch 2] 4 times, (3dc, ch 2, 3dc) in next ch-2 sp, ch 2; rep from * 2 more times, 3dc in next ch-2 sp, ch 2, 2dc into the last ch-2 sp, sl st in second ch of beg ch-4 to join.

Fasten off and secure.

Medium Square
Work Rnds 1–4 of Large Square. Fasten off and secure.

Small Square
Work Rnds 1 and 2 of Large Square. Fasten off and secure.

Bag
Following the list of color sequences at right, make 2 of each square (1 each for bag front and back).

Finishing
Using a whipstitch (see Glossary), sew squares tog as shown at right for the bag front and back. Use a whipstitch to sew the front and back tog along the sides and bottom.

Edging
With A and RS facing, work a row of sc around bag opening, working 1 sc into each dc and 2 sc into each ch-2 sp. Fasten off and secure.

Gusset
Turn bag inside out and flatten base so that the fold is at the center of the base. With A threaded on a tapestry needle, sew a seam across each corner to form "ears" the depth of the small square. Fold "ears" toward center of bag base and lightly stitch in place.

Handle tabs (make 4)
With A, ch 33.

ROW 1: Skip 3 ch, dc in next and all foll ch to end—31 dc.

ROW 2: Ch 3 (counts as 1 dc), dc in first and all foll dc to end.

Fasten off and secure.

Felting
Felt bag and tabs as described in the tips sidebar at right. Pin tabs to a firm surface so that they dry flat and straight.

Attach handles
Pin handle tabs as desired at top edge of bag and insert handles. With A threaded on a needle, sew handle tabs securely to bag.

Lining
Measure bag for lining and add 1" (2.5 cm) to width measurement and 1½" (3.8 cm) to length measurement. Cut two pieces of lining fabric to these measurements. Iron optional patch fabric onto fusible adhesive following manufacturer's directions. Trim to size. Apply message using ink pad and alphabet stamps. Iron patch onto RS of lining fabric in desired location. With contrasting thread and using the buttonhole setting on a sewing machine, topstitch patch in place. With RS facing tog and using a ½" (1.3 cm) seam allowance, sew lining front and back tog along sides and bottom. Press seams. Make gussets as for bag. Fold opened end of lining down 1" (2.5 cm) to WS and press. Pin lining to bag with WS facing and sew in place by hand.

Designs by **MAGS KANDIS** appear in publications including *Interweave Knits, Vogue Knitting, Knitters,* and the Interweave Style book series. She is the editor of *Folk Style.* Mags lives in the heart of Quinte, Ontario.

ASSEMBLY DIAGRAM FOR FRONT AND BACK

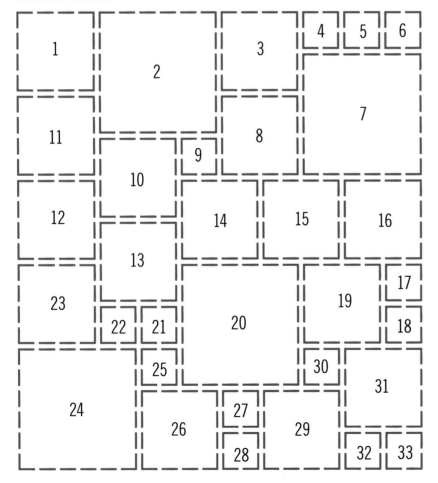

Tips for Felting

- Because every yarn felts differently, it is important that you knit and felt a generous swatch to understand how a particular yarn will behave.

- There is no magical formula when it comes to the shrinking factor of a felted project. Even different colors of the same yarn can produce very different results when washed.

- When felting in the washing machine, place the project in a lingerie bag or pillowcase to reduce the amount of fiber that can escape and clog the machine or attach to the next load of laundry.

- Read the content label to increase your chances of success. If the garment is made of pure wool, 100% wool, lambswool, 100% alpaca, or 50% wool and 50% alpaca; you can expect good results. Blends of these fibers with silk, Tencel, rayon, or soy may also work. Avoid superwash wool, which has been treated not to felt.

- Don't worry about rips or holes—the felting process will prevent them from raveling.

Square	Rnd1	Rnd2	Rnd3	Rnd4	Rnd5	Rnd6
1	C	C	B	B		
2	G	F	F	F	L	L
3	D	D	C	C		
4	J	J				
5	B	L				
6	H	H				
7	L	J	J	J	F	F
8	I	I	I	G		
9	A	A				
10	B	E	E	E		
11	A	I	I	H		
12	D	J	J	J		
13	L	L	L	C		
14	I	I	D	D		
15	E	H	H	J		
16	A	G	G	E		
17	H	L				
18	C	C				
19	L	F	F	F		
20	A	A	I	I	B	B
21	E	E				
22	G	J				
23	B	B	H	H		
24	A	G	G	G	I	I
25	G	G				
26	E	D	D	J		
27	A	A				
28	F	L				
29	G	G	H	H		
30	H	J				
31	D	D	D	G		
32	C	C				
33	B	A				

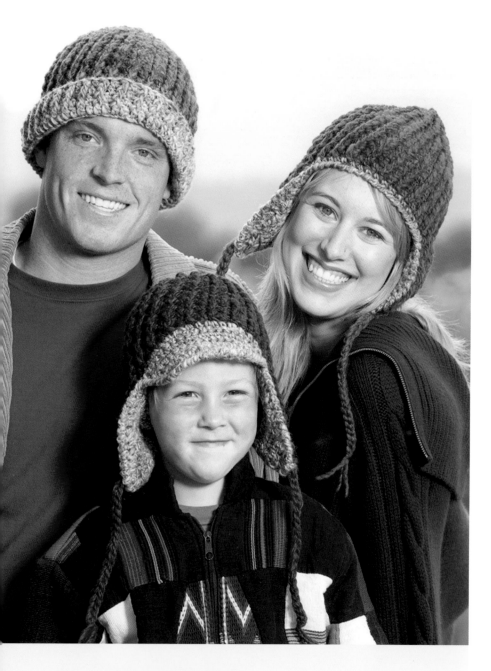

Finished Size
Adult (teen, child) 8½ (8, 7½)" (21.5 [20.5, 19] cm) from top of crown to bottom edge and 23 (20½, 18)" (58.5 [52, 45.5] cm) circumference.

Yarn
Manos del Uruguay Clásica (100% wool; 138 yd [126 m]/3.5 oz [100 g]; (**5**)): #706 (green), 1 skein for adult hat; #704 (red), 2 skeins for teen hat; #708 (blue), 1 skein for child hat (MC); and #703 (gray; CC), 1 skein for all 3 hats. Yarn distributed by Fairmount Fibers.

Hook
Size K/10½ (6.5 mm). Adjust hook size if necessary to obtain correct gauge.

Notions
Yarn needle; stitch marker (m).

Gauge
First 3 rnds of crown = 3½" (9 cm) in diameter.

---

notes

---

* Beg ch 2 counts as hdc on crown only, not on earflaps.
* Pull yarn taut after joining to prevent buckling.

---

stitch guide

Front Post hdc dec (FPhdc dec)
Yo, insert hook around post of next FPdc (see Glossary), yo and pull up lp, yo and draw through 2 lps, insert hook in next hdc, yo and pull up lp, yo draw through all 3 lps on hook.

Increase (inc)
(Hdc, FPdc) in next hdc, (hdc, FPdc) in next FPdc—2 sts inc'd.

Main patt
Hdc in next hdc, FPdc around next FPdc.

Leaf Peeper HATS
by Lisa Soutendijk

Three options in three sizes let you tailor this versatile topper for anyone on your list, incorporating the brim and earflaps as you wish. The contrasting color conjures up sheepskin trapper hats, while the lovely kettle-dyed wool prevents the hat from evoking Elmer Fudd. A clever increasing method, working a half-double and front-post double into the same stitch, gives subtle shaping to this classic hat.

Adult Hat

Crown

RND 1: With MC ch 4 (counts as dc), 11 dc in 4th ch from hook, sl st in top of beg ch-4 to join—12 dc.

RND 2: Ch 2 (counts as a hdc on crown only), FPdc (see Glossary) in same st, [(hdc, FPdc) in next dc] 11 times, sl st in top of beg ch-2 to join—12 hdc, 12 FPdc.

RND 3: Ch 2, FPdc in next st, hdc in next hdc, FPdc in next FPdc, inc (see Stitch Guide), *[hdc in next hdc, FPdc in next FPdc] 2 times, inc; rep from * 3 times, sl st in top of beg ch-2 to join—16 hdc, 16 FPdc.

RND 4: Ch 2, work main patt (see Stitch Guide) around, sl st in top of beg ch-2 to join—16 hdc, 16 FPdc.

RND 5: Ch 2, FPdc in next st, inc, *[hdc in next hdc, FPdc in next FPdc] 3 times, inc; rep from * 3 times, [hdc in next hdc, FPdc in next FPdc] 2 times sl st in top of beg ch-2 to join—20 hdc, 20 FPdc.

RND 6: Rep Rnd 4—20 hdc, 20 FPdc.

RND 7: Ch 2, FPdc in next FPdc, [hdc in next hdc, FPdc in next FPdc] 3 times, inc, *[hdc in next hdc, FPdc in next FPdc] 4 times, inc; rep from * 3 times, sl st in top of beg ch-2 to join—24 hdc, 24 FPdc.

RND 8: Ch 2, FPdc in next FPdc, hdc in next hdc, FPdc in next FPdc, inc, *[hdc in next hdc, FPdc in next FPdc] 5 times, inc; rep from * 3 times, [hdc in next hdc, FPdc in next FPdc] 3 times, sl st in top of beg ch-2 to join—28 hdc, 28 FPdc.

RND 9: Ch 2, FPdc in next FPdc, [hdc in next hdc, FPdc in next FPdc] 5 times, inc, *[hdc in next hdc, FPdc in next FPdc] 6 times, inc; rep from * 3 times, sl st in top of beg ch-2 to join—32 hdc, 32 FPdc.

Rep Rnd 4 until hat measures 8" (20.5 cm) from top of crown to bottom edge. Do not join at end of last rnd, change to CC in last st.

Ribbing

RND 1: With CC, ch 3 (counts as first dc), dc in each st around, sl st in top of beg ch-3 to join, turn—64 dc.

RND 2: (WS) Ch 3, dc through blo (see Glossary) around, sl st in top of beg ch-3 to join, turn—64 dc.

RND 3: Ch 2, [FPdc in next dc, hdc in next dc] 31 times, FPdc in last dc, sl st in top of beg ch-2 to join, do not turn—32 hdc, 32 FPdc.

RNDS 4–5: Ch 2, work main patt, sl st in top of beg ch-2 to join. Fasten off and weave in loose ends.

Fold up ribbing Rnds 2–5, so ribbing is now on RS.

Teen Flap Hat

Crown

Work as for adult hat through Rnd 8—28 hdc, 28 FPdc.

Rep Rnd 4 of adult hat until top of crown to bottom edge measures 7¾" (19.5 cm). Do not fasten off.

Right earflap

ROW 1: Ch 2 (does not count as hdc), hdc in same st, [FPdc in next st, hdc in next st] 7 times, turn—15 sts.

ROW 2: Ch 2, hdc in same st, [BPdc (see Glossary) in next FPdc, hdc in next hdc] 7 times, turn—15 sts.

ROW 3: Ch 2, FPhdc dec (see Stitch Guide), work main patt to last 2 sts, FPhdc dec, turn—13 sts.

ROW 4: Ch 2, hdc2tog (see Glossary), BPdc in each FPdc and hdc in each hdc to last 2 sts, hdc2tog, turn—11 sts.

ROWS 5–8: Rep Rows 3–4—3sts.

ROW 9: Ch 1, sc3tog (see Glossary), before pulling through on last step, take a 3 yd piece of yarn, fold in half, wrap around hook and pull through with working strand.

Ties

With all 3 strands held tog, ch 25 or to length desired. Fasten off and trim ends to 1–2" (2.5–5 cm).

Left earflap

With right earflap on right, RS facing, and counting to left, sk next 17 sts and join in next hdc. Work as for right earflap.

Inner earflap (make 2)

With CC, ch 17.

ROW 1: Hdc in 3rd ch from hook and in each ch across, turn—15 hdc.

ROW 2: Ch 2, hdc in same st and each hdc across, turn—15 hdc.

ROWS 3–8: Ch 2, hdc2tog, hdc to last 2 sts, hdc2tog, turn—3 hdc.

ROW 9: Ch 1, sc3tog. Fasten off and weave in loose ends.

Joining earflaps

Position first inner earflap inside right earflap, join CC with sl st through back corner of right earflap (the same st as beg ch-2) and top corner of Row 1 of inner earflap.

RND 1: Ch 1, sc in same st, *sc through both thicknesses evenly down side edges to point, ch 1, working under tie sc evenly up other side*, sc in each st across front of hat, join 2nd

inner earflap to left earflap as for first earflap, rep from * to *, sc in each st across back, sl st in the first sc to join.

Trim

RND 1: Ch 1, rev sc (see Glossary) around, skipping sc at inner corners of earflaps, sl st in first st to join. Fasten off and weave in loose ends.

Child's Flap Hat

Crown

Work crown as for adult hat through Rnd 7—48 sts. Rep Rnd 4 of adult hat until top of crown to bottom edge measures 7¼" (18.5 cm).

Right earflap

ROW 1: Ch 2, hdc in same st, work even in main patt for 12 more sts, turn—13 sts.

ROW 2: Ch 2, hdc in same st, [BPdc (see Glossary) in next FPdc, hdc in next hdc] 6 times, turn—13 sts.

ROW 3: Ch 2, FPhdc dec (see Stitch Guide) work even in main patt to last 2 sts, FPhdc dec, turn—11 sts.

ROW 4: Ch 2, hdc2tog (see Glossary), *BPdc in next FPdc, hdc in next hdc; rep from * to last 2 sts, hdc2tog, turn—9 sts.

ROWS 5–6: Rep Rows 3–4—5 sts.

ROW 7: Rep Row 3—3 sts.

ROW 8: Rep Row 9 of teen flap hat.

Work ties as for teen hat. Fasten off and weave in loose ends.

Left earflap

Turn hat so right earflap is on right with RS facing, sk 15 sts, join in next hdc. Work as for right earflap.

Inner earflap (make 2)

With CC, ch 15.

ROW 1: Hdc in 3rd ch from hook and in each ch across, turn—13 hdc.

ROW 2: Ch 2, hdc across, turn—13 hdc.

ROWS 3–7: Ch 2, hdc2tog, hdc to last 2 sts, hdc2tog, turn—3 hdc.

ROW 8: Ch 1, sc3tog. Fasten off and weave in loose ends.

Brim

With RS facing, join CC in same st as right earflap, ch 1, sc in next 2 sts, 2 sc in next st, sc in next 2 sts, 2 sc in next st, sc in next 2 sts, 2 sc in next st, sc in next 2 sts, 2 sc in next st, sc in last 3 sts, sl st in same st as beg ch-2 of left earflap, turn—19 sc.

ROW 2: Ch 1, sc across, turn—19 sc.

ROWS 3–5: Ch 1, sc2tog (see Glossary), sc to last 2 sts, sc2tog, turn—13 sc.

ROW 6: Ch 1, sc2tog, sc in next 3 sts, 2 sc in next st, sc in next st, 2 sc in next st, sc in next 3 sts, sc2tog, turn—13 sc.

ROW 7: Rep Row 3, turn—11 sc.

ROW 8: Ch 1, sc2tog, sc in next 3 sts, 2 sc in next st, sc in next 3 sts, sc2tog—10 sc. Fasten off and weave in loose ends.

Joining earflaps

Work join as for teen hat, except work a sc in row-ends of brim and across front, place 2 sc in first and last sc on front of brim.

Trim

Work as for teen hat, working rev sc around brim, sl st in first st to join. Fasten off and weave in all loose ends. 🖋

LISA SOUTENDIJK's grandmother taught her to crochet when she was six. She made her own Barbie doll clothes and finished her first afghan when she was eight. A United States Army veteran, Lisa is very active in donating items to local homeless shelters.

Float Away SCARF
by Kim Werker

From the second I laid eyes on this yarn, it screamed "waves!" A brief dip into *Harmony Guide Basic Crochet Stitches* and a few dangling rings later, this simple scarf was born. Worked in only seven long rows, it's warm enough for chilly spring nights, soft enough to wear against bare skin, and has sheen to add some flair to casual beachwear.

Finished Size

4" × 53½" (10 × 136 cm), including rings (each ring measures 1¼" [3.2 cm] in diameter).

Yarn

Austermann Bambou Soft (65% wool, 35% bamboo; 110 yd [100 m]/1.75 oz [50 g]; (**3**)): #07 teal, 2 balls. Yarn distributed by Skacel.

Hooks

Sizes I/9 (5.5 mm) and H/8 (5 mm). Adjust hook size if necessary to obtain the correct gauge.

Notions

Yarn needle.

Gauge

12 dc and 8 rows = 4" (10 cm) in patt st.

---

note

∗ This scarf uses almost two entire balls of yarn. Gauge is important only in that missed gauge might result in needing a third ball of yarn.

---

stitch guide

Dc2tog

[Yo, insert hook in next st, yo, draw up a lp, yo, draw through 2 lps] 2 times, yo, draw through all lps on hook—1 st dec'd.

Stitch Pattern (multiple of 12 sts + 3)

Row 1: Dc in 5th ch from hook, *dc in each of next 3 ch, [work dc2tog (see Stitch Guide) over next 2 ch] 2 times, dc in each of next 3 ch, [2 dc in next ch] 2 times; rep from *, end with dc in each of next 3 ch, 2 dc in last ch, turn.

Row 2: Ch 4 (counts as first dc), working in back lp only (blo) throughout, dc in first st, *dc in each of next 3 sts, [dc2tog over next 2 sts] 2 times, dc in each of next 3 sts, [2 dc in next st] 2 times; rep from *, end with dc in each of next 3 sts, 2 dc in top of tch, turn.

Rep Row 2 for patt.

Scarf

With larger hook, ch 171. Work Rows 1 and 2 of stitch patt (see Stitch Guide). Rep Row 2 six more times. Fasten off.

Rings (make 6)

With smaller hook, ch 8, join with sl st in first ch to form ring.

RND 1: Ch 1, work 16 sc into ring, sl st in first sc to join, ch 2.

Attach rings (3 evenly spaced across each end of scarf)

With RS of scarf facing, join ch-2 of ring to scarf with sl st around post of dc at end of row. Fasten off.

Finishing

Weave in loose ends. Block lightly. 🌿

KIM WERKER is the author of *Crochet Me,* coauthor of *Teach Yourself Visually Crocheting,* and founder of CrochetMe .com. Formerly the editor of *Interweave Crochet* magazine, she lives in Vancouver, Canada, and blogs at kimwerker.com.

Finished Size

7½ (8, 8¾, 9, 9½, 10½)" (19 [20.5, 22, 23, 24, 26.5] cm) leg circumference. Socks shown measure 9" (23 cm).

Yarn

Universal Yarn Bamboo Sock (50% superwash merino wool, 25% bamboo, 25% nylon; 459 yd [420 m]/3.5 oz [100 g]; (**1**)): #275 deep sea, 1 skein.

Hook

Size D/3 (3.25 mm). Adjust hook size if necessary to obtain correct gauge.

Notions

Stitch markers (m); yarn needle.

Gauge

6½ sh and 16 rows = 4" (10 cm) in sh patt.

----

notes

* Work in the rnd without joining unless otherwise noted, moving m up as instructed.

* Do not fasten off yarn at end of rnds.

* Socks should fit snugly. Due to limited elasticity, sock should be put on and removed gently.

----

stitch guide

Long single crochet (Lsc)
Yo, insert hook in indicated st 1 row below and pull up lp even with working row, yo and draw through both lps on hook.

Shell (sh)
3 dc in indicated st.

Shell patt (multiple of 4 sts)
Set-up row: Sc in 2nd ch from hook, sk next ch, sh (see above) in next ch, *sk next ch, sc in next ch, sk next ch, sh in next ch; rep from * across, turn.

Row 2: Ch 2 (does not count as st), sl st in center dc of first sh, ch 1, sc in same dc, (leave first and last dc of each sh unworked), sh in next sc, *sc in center dc of next sh, sh in next sc; rep from * across, turn.

Rep Row 2 for patt.

Sock

Cuff

RND 1: (RS) Fdc (see Glossary) 38 (42, 42, 46, 50, 54), leaving tail for sewing cuff later and being careful not to twist sts, sl st in 3rd ch of first fdc to join.

RND 2: *BPdc (see Glossary) in 2nd fdc, FPdc in next fdc; rep from *

Adirondack SOCKS

by Patsy Harbor

These socks, perfect for slipping on before hitting the chilly floor in the morning, are fun to make from cuff to toe! The variety of stitches—from the alternating front and back post to the shell leg and extended single-crochet heel—keep you engaged without angst as yarn shifts color from row to row. Best of all, they're very stretchy and comfortable. Our model was planning to make a pair for herself!

around ending with BPdc, do not join or turn (see Notes)—19 (21, 21, 23, 25, 27) BPdc.

Leg

RND 1: Sc in next BPdc, pm in sc just made to mark beg of rnd, sk next st, *sh (see Stitch Guide) in next st, sk next st, sc in next st, sk next st; rep from * around—10 (11, 11, 12, 13, 14) sc, 9 (10, 10, 11, 12, 13) sh.

RND 2: Sh in first sc, move m up to center dc of sh just made, *sc in center dc of next sh (leave first and last dc of each sh unworked, here and throughout), sh in next sc; rep from * around

Rep Rnd 2 moving m each rnd to either sc or center dc of sh until piece measures 6½" (16.5 cm) from beg, ending on a row that ends with a sh. Flatten piece so seam of cuff is at side edge. Mark fold. Work in est patt to side edge (fold point) ending with a sh, turn—5 (5, 5, 6, 7, 7 sh).

Heel

ROW 1: (WS) Ch 1, sc in each dc of first sh, [sc in next sc, sc in each dc of next sh] 3 (4, 4, 5, 6, 7) times, turn leaving rem sts unworked—19 (21, 21, 23, 25, 27) sc.

ROW 2: (RS) Ch 1, sc in first 2 sc, Lsc (see Stitch Guide) in row below next st, *sc in next sc, Lsc in row below next st; rep from * to last 2 sts, sc in last 2 sts, turn.

ROW 3: Ch 1, sc across, turn.

Rep Rows 2–3 until heel measures 2¾" (7 cm), ending on a WS row.

Heel shaping

ROW 1: (RS) Ch 1, sc in first st, sc2tog (see Glossary) 2 times, sc in each st to last 5 sts, sc2tog 2 times, sc in last st, turn—15 (17, 17, 19, 21, 23) sts.

ROW 2: Ch 1, sc in first st, sc2tog, sc in next 4 (5, 5, 5, 6, 6) sts, sc2tog 1 (1, 1, 2, 2, 3) times, sc to last 3 sts, sc2tog, sc in last st, turn—12 (14, 14, 15, 17, 18) sts.

ROW 3: Ch 1, sc in first st, sc2tog, sc in next 0 (3, 3, 4, 5, 5) sts, sc2tog 0 (1, 1, 1, 1, 1) time, sc to last 3 sts, sc2tog, sc in last st, turn—10 (11, 11, 12, 14, 15) sts.

ROW 4: Ch 1, sc in first 4 (4, 4, 5, 6, 6) sts, sc2tog 1 (2, 2, 1, 1, 2) times, sc to end—9 (9, 9, 11, 13, 13) sts.

ROW 5: Sc across—9 (9, 9, 11, 13, 13) sts.

Gusset

RND 1: (RS) Rotate sock 90° to work along side edge of heel flap, work 15 (17, 17, 17, 17, 18) sc evenly spaced along left side edge of heel flap, beg sh patt by working sh in first sc on leg, pm in first dc of sh just made (first gusset m), cont in est sh patt across top of foot to right side edge of heel flap, ending with sh in last sc, pm in last dc of last sh (2nd gusset m), work 15 (17, 17, 17, 17, 18) sc evenly spaced along right side edge of heel flap, esc (see Glossary) in next 9 (9, 9, 11, 13, 13) heel sts, pm in last esc made to mark the beg of rnd—59 (65, 65, 69, 73, 77) sts.

RND 2: Esc to 2 sts before first gusset m, sc2tog, remove m and work next st of sh patt, replace m, work in sh patt to 2nd gusset m, remove m, work next st of sh patt, replace m, sc2tog, esc to end—57 (63, 63, 67, 71, 75) sts.

Rep Rnd 2 until 39 (41, 47, 47, 51, 55) sts rem. Do not fasten off.

Foot

RND 1: Esc to first m, work in sh patt to 2nd m, esc to end—39 (43, 47, 47, 51, 55) sts.

Rep Rnd 1 until sole of sock foot measures 2" (5 cm) less than desired hell-to-toe measurement. Remove rnd m.

Shape toe

Fold sock, making sure heel is centered to back and that markers are at each side edge.

RND 1: Sc in each st to 2 sts from first side m, sc2tog, sc in each st to 2 sts from next side m, sc2tog, sc in next st—37 (41, 45, 45, 49, 53) sc.

RND 2: Sc in each st to 2 sts from first side m, sc2tog, sc in next st, sc2tog, sc in each st to 2 sts from next side m, sc2tog, sc in next st, sc2tog—33 (37, 41, 41, 45, 49) sc.

Rep Rnd 2 until 17 (17, 17, 21, 21, 21) sts rem. Sc in each st to 2 sts from first side m, sc2tog sc in each st to 2 sts from first side m, sc2tog—16 (16, 16, 20, 20, 20) sc. Fasten off and weave in loose ends. Sew toe closed. Sew side seam at cuff opening. ✍

PATSY HARBOR learned to crochet after adopting her second child in 2004 and has not been able to stop since. In addition to designing, she enjoys teaching others to crochet.

Crochet Bobble BERET

by Robyn Chachula

A touch of nostalgic chic makes for a fun, super wearable hat, and this quick-to-crochet project with a knitted ribbing requires little effort for a big payoff. "The fun bobblet stitch creates the bumpy fabric without being bulky," says designer Robyn Chachula.

Size
20" (51 cm) head circumference at brim.

Yarn
Alpaca with a Twist Baby Twist (100% baby alpaca; 110 yd [100 m]/1.75 oz [50 g]): #3003 carnical red, 2 balls

Gauge
19 sts and 24 rows = 4" (10 cm) in st patt.

Tools
Size G/6 (4 mm) crochet hook; size 6 (4 mm): two 16" (40.5 cm) circular (cir) needles; big-eye needle; two ⅝" (1.5 cm) buttons

----

stitch guide

Adjustable ring
Place slipknot on hook, leaving a 4" (10 cm) tail. Wrap tail around fingers to form ring. Work sts of first rnd in ring; at end of first rnd, pull tail to tighten ring.

Bobble
Insert hook into st indicated, yo, pull up a loop, *yo, pull through 1 loop on hook; rep from * once, yo, pull through last 2 loops on hook.

Beret

Form an adjustable ring (see Stitch Guide).

RND 1: (RS) Ch 1, 5 sc into ring, pull ring closed; do not turn.

RND 2: (Sc, bobble) in each sc around; do not turn—10 sts.

RND 3: *Sc in next sc, 2 sc in next sc; rep from * around; do not turn—15 sts.

RND 4: *(Sc, bobble) in next sc, sc in next sc, bobble in next sc; rep from * around—20 sts.

RND 5: *Sc in each of next 3 sc, 2 sc in next sc; rep from * around—25 sts.

RND 6: *(Bobble, sc) in next sc, [bobble in next sc, sc in next sc] twice; rep from * around—30 sts.

RND 7: *Sc in each of next 5 sc, 2 sc in next sc; rep from * around—35 sts.

RND 8: *(Sc, bobble) in next sc, [sc in next sc, bobble in next sc] 3 times; rep from * around—40 sts.

RND 9: *Sc in each of next 7 sc, 2 sc in next sc; rep from * around—45 sts.

RND 10: *(Bobble, sc) in next sc, [bobble in next sc, sc in next sc] 4 times; rep from * around—50 sts.

RND 34: *Sc2tog over next 2 sc, bobble in next sc, [sc in next sc, bobble in next sc] 9 times—100 sts rem.

RND 35: *Sc in each of next 18 sc, sc2tog over next 2 sc; rep from * around—95 sts rem. Fasten off.

Finishing

With two cir needles, pick up and knit 95 sts evenly around brim. Join in the rnd.

NEXT RND: *K4, p1; rep from * around.

Work 5 more rnds in rib. BO all sts loosely. Weave in ends. Sew two decorative buttons to brim as desired. 🍃

ROBYN CHACHULA'S book, *Unexpected Afghans* (Interweave, 2012) shows how to use classic crochet techniques for astoundingly innovative afghans. She is grateful to be able to design and write from home in Pittsburgh, Pennsylvania, while playing with her little "office assistants." She is also the author of *Blueprint Crochet, Baby Blueprint Crochet,* and *Simply Crochet* (all from Interweave) and *Crochet Stitches Visual Encyclopedia* (Wiley, 2011).

RND 11: *Sc in each of next 9 sc, 2 sc in next sc; rep from * around—55 sts.

RND 12: *(Sc, bobble) in next sc, [sc in next sc, bobble in next sc] 5 times; rep from * around—60 sts.

RND 13: *Sc in each of next 11 sc, 2 sc in next sc; rep from * around—65 sts.

RND 14: *(Bobble, sc) in next sc, [bobble in next sc, sc in next sc] 6 times; rep from * around—70 sts.

RND 15: *Sc in each of next 13 sc, 2 sc in next sc; rep from * around—75 sts.

RND 16: *(Sc, bobble) in next sc, [sc in next sc, bobble in next sc] 7 times; rep from * around—80 sts.

RND 17: *Sc in each of next 15 sc, 2 sc in next sc; rep from * around—85 sts.

RND 18: *(Bobble, sc) in next sc, [bobble in next sc, sc in next sc] 8 times; rep from * around—90 sts.

RND 19: *Sc in each of next 17 sc, 2 sc in next sc; rep from * around—95 sts.

RND 20: *(Sc, bobble) in next sc, [sc in next sc, bobble in next sc] 9 times; rep from * around—100 sts.

RND 21: *Sc in each of next 19 sc, 2 sc in next sc; rep from * around—105 sts.

RND 22: *(Bobble, sc) in next sc, [bobble in next sc, sc in next sc] 10 times; rep from * around—110 sts.

RND 23: Sc in each sc around.

RND 24: *Sc in next sc, bobble in next sc; rep from * around.

RND 25: Rep Rnd 23.

RNDS 26–32: *Bobble in next sc, sc in next sc; rep from * around.

Rep Rnds 23–26 once more, then Rep Rnds 23–24 once.

RND 33: *Sc in each of next 20 sc, sc2tog over next 2 sc; rep from * around—105 sts rem.

Breezy HAT

by Linda Permann

This openwork hat has the right amount of warmth if you're in cooler climates and the right amount of cool for hanging with your peeps. The asymmetrical shells are worked in the round in a rainbow of colors for a fun effect. Try working it in a single color for a more sophisticated look.

Finished Size

21" (53.5 cm) circumference to fit average woman's head.

Yarn

Lion Brand Cotton Ease (50% cotton, 50% acrylic; 207 yd [108 m]/3.5 oz [100 g]; (4)): #194 lime (A), #100 snow (B), #186 maize (C), #148 turquoise (D), #134 terracotta (E), and #195 azalea (F), 1 ball each. **NOTE:** To make hat in 1 color, use 1 ball of any color.

Hook

Size G/6 (4 mm). Adjust hook size if necessary to obtain correct gauge.

Notions

Yarn needle.

Gauge

First 2 rnds measure 3¼" (8.5 cm) in diameter.

---

stitch guide

Adjustable ring

Place slipknot on hook, leaving 4" (10 cm) tail. Wrap tail around fingers 1 time to form ring. Work sts of first rnd in ring. At end of first rnd, pull tail to tighten ring.

Hat

With A, make adjustable ring (see Stitch Guide).

RND 1: Ch 3 (counts as dc throughout), 9 dc in ring changing to B in last dc, sl st in 3rd ch of beg ch-3 to join—10 dc.

RND 2: Ch 3, dc in first st, 2 dc in each of next 9 sts changing to C in last dc, sl st in 3rd ch of beg ch-3 to join—20 dc.

RND 3: Ch 3, [2 dc in next dc, dc in next dc] 9 times, 2 dc in last dc changing to D in last dc, sl st in 3rd ch of beg ch-3 to join—30 dc.

RND 4: Ch 5 (counts as dc and ch 2), dc in first st, dc in next 4 dc, ch 2, *(dc, ch 2, dc) in next dc, dc in next 4 dc, ch 2; rep from * 4 more times, sl st in beg ch-3 to join—36 dc, 12 ch-2 sps. Fasten off.

RND 5: Join E in last ch-2 sp of Rnd 4, ch 3, (3 dc, ch 2, dc) in same ch-2 sp, dc in next ch-2 sp, sk 2 dc, (dc, ch 2, dc) in next dc, sk 2 dc, *(4 dc, ch 2, dc) in next ch-2 sp, dc in next ch-2 sp, sk 2 dc, (dc, ch 2, dc) in next dc, sk 2 dc; rep from * 4 more times, sl st in top of beg ch-3 to join—48 dc, 12 ch-2 sps. Fasten off.

RND 6: Join F in any ch-2 sp, (ch 3, 3 dc, ch 2, dc) in same ch-2 sp, (4 dc, ch 2, dc) in each ch-2 sp around, sl st in top of beg ch-3 to join—60 dc. Fasten off.

RNDS 7–13: Rep Row 6 working color sequence A, B, C, D, E, F, A.

RND 14: Join B in 3rd dc of any 4 dc cluster, *sk (dc, ch 2, dc), 5 dc in next dc, sk next dc, sl st in next dc; rep from * 11 more times, working last sl st in dc yarn was joined in, sl st in first dc to join—60 dc. Fasten off and weave in loose ends. ✿

LINDA PERMANN is a crochet and craft designer who lives in Bozeman, Montana. She is the author of *Crochet Adorned: Reinvent Your Wardrobe with Crocheted Accents, Embellishments, and Trims* (Potter Craft, 2009). See more of her work at www.lindamade.com.

Boteh SCARF

by Kathy Merrick

This simple motif reminds designer Kathy Merrick of Persian carpet *Boteh* (Old Persian for "cluster of leaves"). Boteh can look like leaves, pine cones, pears, or paisleys. Each motif flows gracefully into the next, resulting in a swirled effect, and this lightweight wool yarn lends excellent drape to the whole project.

Finished Size
About 4½" × 72" (11.5 × 183 cm).

Yarn
Lorna's Laces Shepherd Sock (80% superwash wool, 20% nylon; 215 yd [190 m]/1.75 oz [50 g]): chino, 2 skeins.

Hook
Size F/5 (3.75 mm). Adjust hook size if necessary to obtain correct gauge.

Notions
Yarn needle.

Gauge
24 sts and 15 rows = 4" (10 cm) in hdc.

notes

* This is a modular scarf made of curved triangular pieces joined by rows of double-treble crochet worked down the angled (decreased) side of each piece.

* To keep your rows of hdc even, be sure to work the stitch directly below the turning chain at the beginning of each row. When you reach the end of the row, do not work a stitch in the turning chain from the row below.

stitch guide

Dtr
Yo 3 times, insert hook in next st, yo and draw up a lp (5 lps on hook), [yo and draw through first 2 lps on hook] 4 times.

First Triangle
(see stitch diagram at right)

Ch 17.

ROW 1: Hdc in 3rd ch from hook and in each ch across, turn—15 hdc.

ROW 2: (WS) Ch 2, work 1 row hdc, turn.

ROW 3: (RS) Ch 2, hdc in each st across to last hdc, turn, leaving last hdc unworked.

ROW 4: (WS) Ch 2, hdc in each hdc of previous row.

Rep Rows 2 and 3, leaving the last st unworked on each RS row, until you have a row with only 1 st—29 rows total. Hdc in next st, then turn and work 1 hdc in st just worked; turn to work down the side (dec) edge of piece as foll:

DTR ROW: Ch 5, dtr (see Stitch Guide) in tch of Row 28 then work 1 dtr in tch of every other row including fdn ch—15 dtr; turn.

Second Triangle
See stitch diagram below.

Ch 2. Work as for first triangle, beg with Row 2. Work second triangle 15 times for a total of 16 triangles. Fasten off.

Finishing
Join yarn and work 1 row hdc evenly (about 2 hdc for every 3 rows) around the entire scarf. Fasten off. Weave in loose ends. Steam-block lightly to smooth out scarf if needed. 🌿

KATHY MERRICK lives in New Hope, Pennsylvania, where she thinks she is only dreaming that she works for quilt artist Liza Prior Lucy.

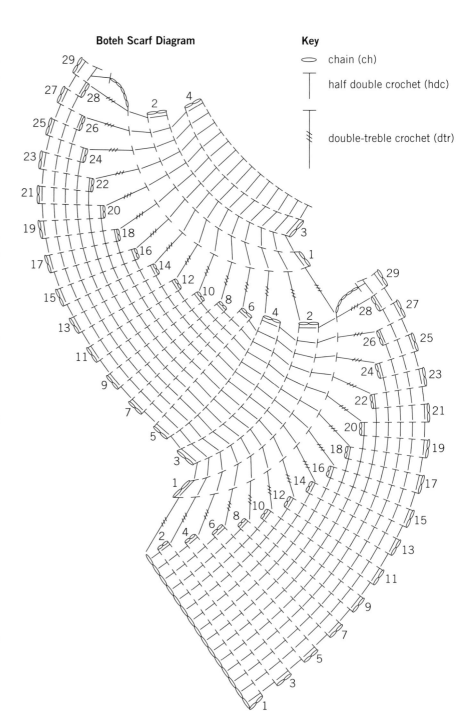

Boteh Scarf Diagram

Key
⌒ chain (ch)
| half double crochet (hdc)
‡ double-treble crochet (dtr)

Marigold HEADBAND
by Sarah Read

Catherine Wheel stitch creates a sunny crocheted headband to hold your tresses. The sample shown is worked in size 10 thread, but this easy accessory can be worked with any weight yarn or number of rows for fun modifications. Try working this headband in a single color or play with combining multiple colors for a variety of looks.

Finished Size
22" (56 cm) head circumference, 2½" (6.5 cm) wide at center front.

Yarn
Nazli Gelin Garden size 10 (100% mercerized cotton; 308 yd [282 m]/1.75 oz [50 g]; (10)): #700-06 (red; MC); #700-04 (yellow; CC); 1 ball each. Yarn distributed by Universal Yarn.

Hook
Size 7 (1.50 mm) steel hook. Adjust hook size if necessary to obtain correct gauge.

Notions
Yarn needle; elastic hair band; st markers (m; optional).

Gauge
36 st and 56 rows = 4" (10 cm) in sc.

---

notes

* Headband is worked end to end; shaping is done with changing height of sts.

* Place markers (m), if desired, in the top of each cl.

* To start next color, draw new color through last 2 lps of last sc in previous row, drop old color, ch 1, turn. Carry previous color along row-end to be picked up at next color change.

---

stitch guide

5 double crochet cluster (5-dc cl)
[Yo, insert hook in next st, yo and pull up lp, yo and draw through 2 lps] 5 times, yo and draw through all 6 lps on hook.

9 double crochet cluster (9-dc cl)
[Yo, insert hook in next st, yo and pull up lp, yo and draw through 2 lps] 9 times, yo and draw through all 10 lps on hook.

Pattern

With MC, ch 170.

ROW 1: (RS) Sc in 2nd ch from hook and in next 19 ch, hdc in next 10 ch, dc in next 11 ch, [sk 3 ch, 9 dc in next ch, sk 3 ch*, sc in next ch] 11 times, ending last rep at *, dc in next 11 ch, hdc in next 10 ch, sc in rem 20 ch, change to CC in last sc, turn—191 sts.

ROW 2: Ch 1, sc in first 20 sc, hdc in next 10 hdc, dc in next 10 dc, ch 1, 5-dc cl (see Stitch Guide), [ch 3, sc in next dc, ch 3*, 9-dc cl (see Stitch Guide)] 11 times, ending last rep at *, 5-dc cl, ch 1, dc in next 10 dc,

hdc in next 10 hdc, sc in rem 20 sts, turn.

ROW 3: Ch 1, sc in first 20 sc, hdc in next 10 hdc, dc in next 10 dc, 5 dc in next cl, sc in next sc, [9 dc in next cl, sc in next sc] 10 times, 5 dc in next cl, dc in next 10 dc, hdc in next 10 hdc, sc in rem 20 sc, change to MC in last sc, turn—191 sts.

ROW 4: Ch 1, sc in first 20 sc, hdc in next 10 hdc, dc in next 11 dc, [ch 3, 9-dc cl, ch 3*, sc in next dc] 11 times, ending last rep at *, dc in next 11 dc, hdc in next 10 hdc, sc in rem 20 sc, turn.

ROW 5: Ch 1, sc in first 20 sc, hdc in next 10 hdc, dc in next 11 dc, [9 dc in next cl, sc in next sc] 11 times,

dc in next 11 dc, hdc in next 10 hdc, sc in rem 20 sc, change to CC in last sc, turn—191 sts.

ROWS 6–12: Rep Rows 2–5, then Rows 2–4. Fasten off, leaving a long tail.

Finishing

With yarn tails, whipstitch (see Glossary) elastic band to row-ends of one end, twist elastic band into a figure eight, whipstitch other side of elastic band to other end of head-band. Weave in ends. Block lightly. 🌿

SARAH READ, the project editor for *Interweave Crochet*, maintains that yarn is an excellent insulator for one's home.

Designer Tips

Carry unused color of yarn up one end of the project to avoid having to weave in too many ends. You can adjust the size of the head-band by adding or subtracting single crochets from the row-ends. This project can be worked in any weight of yarn. Try working it in worsted weight, with fewer single crochets and fewer rows, for a cozy earwarmer.

Stitch Key

⬯ = ch (chain)

✕ = sc (single crochet)

┬ = dc (double crochet)

⟍⟋ = 5-dc cl (5 double crochet cluster)

⟍⟋ = 9-dc cl (9 double crochet cluster)

Pattern Repeat

Finished Size
About 66" (168 cm) long and 8"
(20.5 cm) wide.

Yarn
Sportweight (#2 fine).

Shown here: Alchemy Silken Straw
(100% silk; 260 yd [237 m]/40 g):
#67e topaz, 1 skein.

Hook
Size 7 (4.5 mm).

Notions
Tapestry needle (with eye big enough to
thread the yarn yet small enough for the
beads to slide over); 252 size 6° silver-
colored glass seed beads.

Gauge
About 7 grids = 4" (10 cm) wide and
5" (12.5 cm) high. Exact gauge is not
crucial for this project.

----

notes

* The pattern is a multiple of 4 stitches
  plus 11.

* Leave a length of yarn about 30"
  (76 cm) long at beginning of piece
  to use later for stringing beads.

Scarf

Leaving a 30" (76 cm) tail (to use later
to string beads), ch 63.

ROW 1: Trc into eleventh ch from
hook, *ch 3, sk 3 ch, trc into next
ch; rep from * to end, turn—14
grids.

ROW 2: Ch 7 (counts as 1 trc and 3 ch),
*trc in top of the next trc, ch 3; rep
from * to last grid, sk 3 ch, trc in
next ch, turn.

Rep Row 2 until piece measures 66"
(168 cm) or desired length, leaving a
minimum of 30" (76 cm) of yarn for
stringing beads.

Fasten off and secure.

Finishing

Thread yarn still attached to piece
onto tapestry needle. *Slide 9 beads
onto yarn. Secure beaded "scallop"
with a few stitches at the base of the
next trc; rep from * to end. Fasten off
securely and weave in end. Rep for
opposite edge.

Block to measurements.

Gilded Mesh SCARF
by Mags Kandis

The simple stitch used for this project combined with the crisp
ribbonlike silk yarn will make even a newbie crocheter look like a
pro. In just a few easy evenings, a luscious length of spun gold
will magically flow from your hook. Add a scalloped edge of silver
beads to take the opulence one step further. If your recipient is
not a flashy gal, try a dry linen or a raw silk yarn and trim the
ends with beads that have a subtle matte finish.

Cheerful EARMUFFS
by Mags Kandis

Those who live in cold climates know that combating chilly ears in a stylish way can take a lot of imagination—especially when avoiding "hat head." Ears will stay toasty and passersby will smile when these quirky muffs appear. I reclaimed the frame from fake fur muffs that had knocked around my closet for far too long. If you don't have your own old frame, take a trip to a local rummage shop. Who knows what else you can find there that will inspire you for other projects?

Finished Size
Inside frame measures 3" (7.5 cm) in diameter at the ears.

Yarn
DK weight (#3 Fine).

Shown here: Classic Elite Miracle (50% alpaca, 50% Tencel; 108 yd [99 m]/50 g): #3318 olive, 1 skein. This yarn has been discontinued; substitute the DK weight yarn of your choice.

Hook
Size G/6 (4 mm). Adjust hook size if necessary to obtain the correct gauge.

Notions
Earmuffs frame (reclaimed, if possible); tapestry needle; small amount of polyester or bamboo fiber filling.

Gauge
18 dc and 4 rows = 4" (10 cm).

Muff Inside Piece (make 2)

RND 1: Ch 2, 6 sc in second ch from hook, sl st in first ch to join—6 sc.

RND 2: Ch 1 (counts as 1 sc), sc in same ch, [2 sc in next sc] 5 times, sl st in top of ch-1 to join—12 sc.

RNDS 3, 5, 7, AND 9: Ch 1, sc into each sc, sl st in top of ch-1 to join.

RND 4: Ch 1, sc in same ch, [2 sc in next sc] 11 times, sl st in top of ch-1 to join—24 sc.

RND 6: Ch 1, 1 sc into same ch, sc into next sc; *2 sc into next sc, sc into next sc; rep from * to end, sl st in top of ch-1 to join—36 sc.

RND 8: Ch 1, 1 sc into same ch, sc into the next 2 sc, *2 sc into next sc, sc into next 2 sc; rep from * to end, sl st in top of ch-1 to join—48 sc.

Fasten off and secure.

Muff Outside Piece (make 2)

RNDS 1–8: Work as for inside piece.

RND 9: Ch 5, sl st in same ch-1 as join of previous rnd, *ch 5, sl st in next sc; rep from * to end.

Fasten off and secure.

Band Cover

Ch 12, turn.

ROW 1: Skip 3 ch, dc in each ch to end, turn—10 dc.

ROW 2: Ch 2 (counts as dc), dc in each dc to end, turn.

Rep Row 2 until piece measures about 12½" (31.5 cm) from beg or long enough to cover band of earmuff frame.

Fasten off and secure.

Flowers (make 6)

RND 1: Ch 2, 5 sc in second ch from hook, sl st in top of first sc.

RND 2: Ch 2, (3dc, ch 2, sl st) in the same sc as joining sl st, *ch 2, (3dc, ch 2, sl st) into next sc; rep from * 3 more times—5 petals.

Fasten off.

Danglies

Dangly 1

Work Rnds 1 and 2 of flower but do not fasten off. Ch 20, turn, skip first ch, sl st in each ch to end.

Fasten off.

Dangly 2

Work Rnds 1 and 2 of flower but do not fasten off. Ch 15, turn, skip first ch, sl st in each ch to end.

Fasten off.

Dangly 3

Work Rnds 1 and 2 of flower but do not fasten off. Ch 10, turn, skip first ch, sl st in each ch to end.

Fasten off.

Finishing

Wrap band cover around earmuff frame band and, with yarn threaded on a tapestry needle, use a mattress stitch to join side edges tog. With WS facing, sew one inside piece to one outside piece, leaving about one-third of the distance open. Insert round wired part of earmuff frame, lightly stuff, then sew to end of seam. Rep for other side. Sew ends of band cover to earmuff sections. Sew flowers evenly spaced along band.

Attach danglies in a group near the band join at the top of one earmuff. 🌿

Abbreviations

beg	begin(s); beginning		**patt(s)**	pattern(s)
bet	between		**pm**	place marker
blo	back loop only		**p**	purl
CC	contrasting color		**rem**	remain(s); remaining
ch	chain		**rep**	repeat; repeating
cm	centimeter(s)		**rev sc**	reverse single crochet
cont	continue(s); continuing		**rnd(s)**	round(s)
dc	double crochet		**RS**	right side
dtr	double treble crochet		**sc**	single crochet
dec(s)('d)	decrease(s); decreasing; decreased		**sk**	skip
est	established		**sl**	slip
fdc	foundation double crochet		**sl st**	slip(ped) stitch
flo	front loop only		**sp(s)**	space(es)
foll	follows; following		**st(s)**	stitch(es)
fsc	foundation single crochet		**tch**	turning chain
g	gram(s)		**tog**	together
hdc	half double crochet		**tr**	treble crochet
inc(s)('d)	increase(s); increasing; increased		**WS**	wrong side
k	knit		**yd**	yard
lp(s)	loop(s)		**yo**	yarn over hook
MC	main color		*****	repeat starting point
m	marker		**( )**	alternate measurements and/or instructions
mm	millimeter(s)		**[ ]**	work bracketed instructions a specified number of times

Standard Yarn Weight System

 0 LACE
Yarn: Fingering, 10-count crochet thread
Gauge: 33–40 sts
Hook (metric): 1.5–2.25 mm
Hook (U.S.): 000 to 1

 1 SUPERFINE
Yarn: Sock, Fingering, Baby
Gauge: 21–32 sts
Hook (metric): 2.25–3.5 mm
Hook (U.S.): B-1 to E-4

 2 FINE
Yarn: Sport, Baby
Gauge: 16–20 sts
Hook (metric): 3.5–4.5 mm
Hook (U.S.): E-4 to G-7

 3 LIGHT
Yarn: DK, Light Worsted
Gauge: 12–17 sts
Hook (metric): 3.5–4.5 mm
Hook (U.S.): G-7 to I-9

 4 MEDIUM
Yarn: Worsted, Afghan, Aran
Gauge: 11–14 sts
Hook (metric): 5.5–6.5 mm
Hook (U.S.): I-9 to K-10½

 5 BULKY
Yarn: Chunky, Craft, Rug
Gauge: 8–11 sts
Hook (metric): 6.5–9 mm
Hook (U.S.): K-10½ to M-13

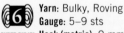 **6** SUPER BULKY
Yarn: Bulky, Roving
Gauge: 5–9 sts
Hook (metric): 9 mm and larger
Hook (U.S.): M-13 and larger

Crochet Gauge

To check gauge, chain 30 to 40 stitches using recommended hook size. Work in pattern stitch until piece measures at least 4" (10 cm) from foundation chain. Lay swatch on flat surface. Place a ruler over swatch and count number of stitches across and number of rows down (including fractions of stitches and rows) in 4" (10 cm). Repeat two or three times on different areas of swatch to confirm measurements. If you have more stitches and rows than called for in instructions, use a larger hook; if you have fewer, use a smaller hook. Repeat until gauge is correct.

Glossary

Learn to Crochet

Chain (ch)

Make a slipknot on hook, *yarn over and draw through loop of slipknot; repeat from * drawing yarn through last loop formed.

Slip Stitch (sl st)

*Insert hook in stitch, yarn over and draw loop through stitch and loop on hook; repeat from *.

Single Crochet (sc)

*Insert hook in stitch, yarn over and pull up loop (**figure 1**), yarn over and draw through both loops on hook (**figure 2**); repeat from *.

FIGURE 1   FIGURE 2

Half Double Crochet (hdc)

*Yarn over, insert hook in stitch, yarn over and pull up loop (3 loops on hook), yarn over (**figure 1**) and draw through all loops on hook (**figure 2**); repeat from *.

FIGURE 1   FIGURE 2

Double Crochet (dc)

*Yarn over, insert hook in stitch, yarn over and pull up loop (3 loops on hook; **figure 1**), yarn over and draw through 2 loops (**figure 2**), yarn over and draw through remaining 2 loops (**figure 3**); repeat from *.

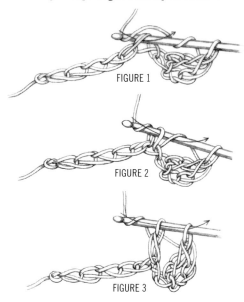

FIGURE 1

FIGURE 2

FIGURE 3

Treble Crochet (tr)

*Yarn over 2 times, insert hook in stitch, yarn over and pull up loop (4 loops on hook; **figure 1**), yarn over and draw through 2 loops (**figure 2**), yarn over and draw through 2 loops, yarn over and draw through remaining 2 loops (**figure 3**); repeat from *.

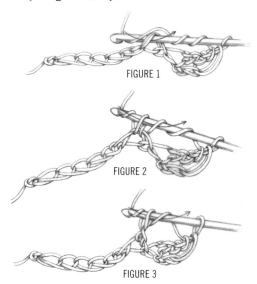

FIGURE 1

FIGURE 2

FIGURE 3

Adjustable Loop

Place slipknot on hook, leaving a 4" (10 cm) tail. Wrap tail around fingers to form ring. Work stitches of first round into ring. At end of first round, pull tail to tighten ring.

Adjustable Ring

Make a large loop with the yarn (**figure 1**). Holding the loop with your fingers, insert hook into loop and pull working yarn through loop (**figure 2**). Yarn over hook, pull through loop on hook.

Continue to work indicated number of stitches into loop (**figure 3**; shown in single crochet). Pull on yarn tail to close loop (**figure 4**).

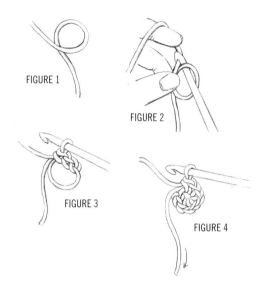

FIGURE 1

FIGURE 2

FIGURE 3

FIGURE 4

Back Post Double Crochet (BPdc)

Yarn over, insert hook from back to front to back around post of stitch to be worked, yarn over and pull up loop [yarn over, draw through 2 loops on hook] 2 times.

Back Loop Only (blo)

Insert the hook between the strands of the "V" and under the loop on the back side of the work. Fabric worked blo has a ridge in it and has more stretch than fabric worked otherwise. It's often used for ribbing.

Double Crochet Two Together (dc2tog)

[Yarn over, insert hook in next stitch, yarn over and pull up loop, yarn over and draw through 2 loops] 2 times, yarn over and draw through all loops on hook—1 stitch decreased.

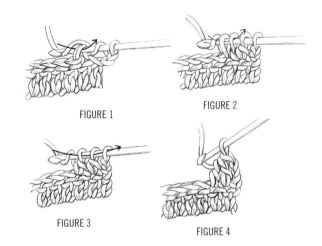

FIGURE 1

FIGURE 2

FIGURE 3

FIGURE 4

Double Crochet Three Together (dc3tog)

[Yarn over, insert hook in next stitch, yarn over and pull up loop, yarn over and draw through 2 loops] 3 times (4 loops on hook), yarn over and draw through all loops on hook—2 stitches decreased.

Double Crochet Four Together (dc4tog)

[Yarn over, insert hook in next stitch, yarn over and pull up loop, yarn over and draw through 2 loops] 4 times, yarn over, draw through all loops on hook—3 stitches decreased.

Extended Single Crochet (esc)

Insert hook in next stitch or chain, yarn over and pull up loop (2 loops on hook), yarn over and draw through 1 loop (1 chain made), yarn over and pull through 2 loops—1 esc completed.

Front Loop Only (flo)

Insert the hook under the strand of the "V" that is closest to you. Fabric worked flo is flatter and taller than fabric worked otherwise.

Foundation Single Crochet (fsc)

Ch 2 **(figure 1)**, insert hook in 2nd ch from hook **(figure 2)**, yarn over hook and draw up a loop (2 loops on hook), yarn over hook, draw yarn through first loop on hook **(figure 3)**, yarn over hook and draw through 2 loops on hook **(figure 4)**—1 fsc made **(figure 5)**. *Insert hook under 2 loops of ch made at base of previous stitch **(figure 6)**, yarn over hook and draw up a loop (2 loops on hook), yarn over hook and draw through first loop on hook, yarn over hook and draw through 2 loops on hook **(figure 7)**. Repeat from * for length of foundation.

Foundation Double Crochet (fdc)

Chain 3. Yarn over, insert hook in 3rd chain from hook, yarn over and pull up loop (3 loops on hook), yarn over and draw through 1 loop (1 chain made), [yarn over and draw through 2 loops] 2 times **(figure 1)**—1 foundation double crochet. Yarn over, insert hook under the 2 loops of the chain at the bottom of the stitch just made, yarn over and pull up loop (3 loops on hook) **(figure 2)**, yarn over and draw through 1 loop (1 chain made), [yarn over and draw through 2 loops] 2 times **(figure 3)**. *Yarn over, insert hook under the 2 loops of the chain at the bottom of the stitch just made **(figure 4)**, yarn over and pull up loop (3 loops on hook), yarn over and draw through 1 loop (1 chain made), [yarn over and draw through 2 loops] 2 times. Repeat from * **(figure 5)**.

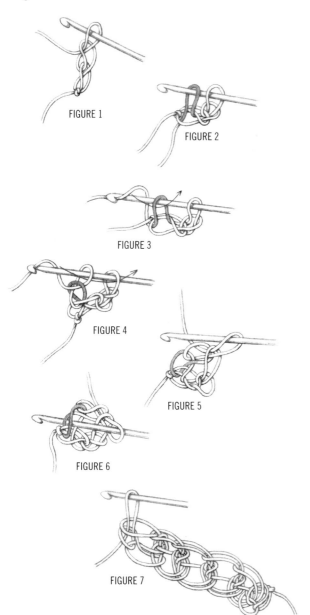

FIGURE 1

FIGURE 2

FIGURE 3

FIGURE 4

FIGURE 5

FIGURE 6

FIGURE 7

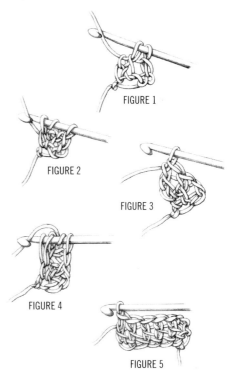

FIGURE 1

FIGURE 2

FIGURE 3

FIGURE 4

FIGURE 5

Front Post Double Crochet (FPdc)

Yarn over, insert hook from front to back to front around post of stitch to be worked, yarn over and pull up loop [yarn over and draw through 2 loops on hook] 2 times.

Front Post Double Treble (FPdtr)

Yarn over 3 times, insert hook from front to back to front around the post of the indicated stitch below, yarn over and pull up loop [yarn over, draw through 2 loops on hook] 4 times.

Front Post Single Crochet (FPsc)

Insert hook from front to back to front around the post of corresponding stitch below, yarn over and pull up loop, yarn over and draw through both loops on hook.

Front Post Treble Crochet (FPtr)

Yarn over 2 times, insert hook from front to back to front around the post of the corresponding stitch below, yarn over and pull up loop [yarn over, draw through 2 loops on hook] 3 times.

Half Double Crochet Two Together (hdc2tog)

[Yarn over, insert hook in next stitch, yarn over and pull up loop] 2 times (5 loops on hook), yarn over and draw through all loops on hook—1 stitch decreased.

Reverse Single Crochet (rev sc)

Working from left to right, insert crochet hook in an edge stitch and pull up loop, yarn over and draw this loop through the first one to join, *insert hook in next stitch to right **(figure 1)**, pull up a loop, yarn over **(figure 2)**, and draw through both loops on hook **(figure 3)**; repeat from *.

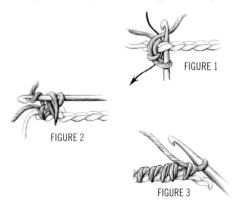

FIGURE 1

FIGURE 2

FIGURE 3

Single Crochet Two Together (sc2tog)

Insert hook into stitch and draw up a loop. Insert hook into next stitch and draw up a loop. Yarn over hook **(figure 1)**. Draw through all 3 loops on hook **(figures 2 and 3)**.

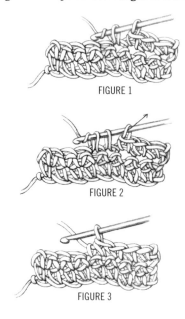

FIGURE 1

FIGURE 2

FIGURE 3

Single Crochet Three Together (sc3tog)

[Insert hook in next stitch, yarn over, pull loop through stitch] 3 times (4 loops on hook). Yarn over and draw yarn through all four loops on hook. Completed sc3tog—2 stitches decreased.

Slip-Stitch Crochet Seam

Make a slipknot with seaming yarn and place on hook. With RS of pieces facing each other, *insert hook through both pieces of fabric under the stitch loops, wrap yarn around hook to form a loop **(figure 1)**, and pull loop back through both pieces of fabric and through the loop already on hook **(figure 2)**. Repeat from *, maintaining firm, even tension.

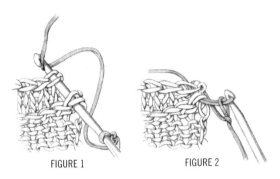

FIGURE 1   FIGURE 2

Whipstitch Seam

Place pieces with right sides together. Hold pieces with the 2 edges facing you.

STEP 1: Secure seaming yarn on wrong side of one piece. Pass needle through pieces from back to front at start of seam. This creates a small stitch to begin seam.

STEP 2: A little farther left, pass needle through pieces, again from back to front, wrapping seam edge.

Repeat Step 2 to complete seam. Secure end of seaming yarn.

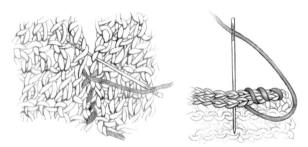

Woven Seam

Place pieces side by side on a flat surface, right sides facing you and the edges lined up row by row or stitch by stitch.

STEP 1: Secure seaming yarn on wrong side of piece A at start of seam. Pass needle to right side at bottom of first stitch.

STEP 2: Put needle through bottom of first stitch of piece B and pass it up to right side again at top of stitch (or in stitch above, if you're working in single crochet).

STEP 3: Put needle through bottom of first stitch of piece A, exactly where you previously passed needle to right side, and bring needle to right side at top of same stitch.

STEP 4: Put needle through piece B where you previously passed needle to right side, and bring needle to right side at the top of same or next stitch.

STEP 5: Put the needle through piece A, where you previously passed needle to right side, and bring needle through to right side at top of stitch.

Repeat Steps 4 and 5, gently tightening seam as you go, being careful not to distort fabric. Allow rows to line up but don't make seam tighter than edges themselves. Edges will roll to the wrong side of work. Secure end of seaming yarn.

PIECE A   PIECE B

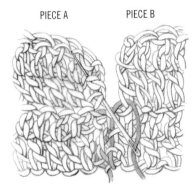

Woven seam applied "row to row"

Find popular patterns for quick and easy projects with these *Craft Tree* publications, brought to you by Interweave.

Crocheted Afghans
ISBN 978-1-62033-094-4

Crocheted Amigurumi
ISBN 978-1-62033-093-7

Crocheted Baby Gifts
ISBN 978-1-59668-739-4

Easy Crocheted Accessories
ISBN 978-1-59668-738-7

Easy Knitted Accessories
ISBN 978-1-62033-092-0

Easy Knitted Hats
ISBN 978-1-62033-097-5

Visit your favorite retailer or order online at interweavestore.com

INTERWEAVE.
interweavestore.com